P9-CQM-292

* * *

ESSENTIAL

[paint techniques]

improving your home with paint

[contents]

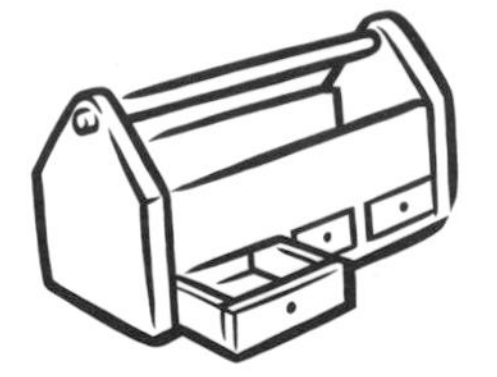

THIS OLD HOUSE ®
ESSENTIAL PAINT
TECHNIQUES,
A *THIS OLD HOUSE* ® BOOK
BY THE EDITORS OF
THIS OLD HOUSE MAGAZINE

PRINTED IN THE UNITED
STATES OF AMERICA
NEW YORK, NEW YORK

FIRST EDITION
ISBN 0-9666753-2-0

10 9 8 7 6 5 4 3 2 1

COVER PHOTOGRAPHY:
JIM COOPER

Library of Congress Cataloging-in-Publication Data
Essential paint techniques. Improving your home with paint.
p. cm.
ISBN 0-9666753-2-0 (alk. paper)
1. House painting Amateurs' manuals. I. This Old House Books.
TT324. E84 1999 99-22950
698' .1—dc21 CIP

[introduction]

PAINTING IS THE CONSTRUCTION ART MOST PEOPLE ARE HANDS-ON familiar with. The tools of the trade are simple and inexpensive, and the rewards of painting are immediate and profound. Paint dark walls white, for example, and you'll be awed by the impact of color on your perception of space. The right color can warm a cold room; a clever technique can raise a low ceiling or lower a high one. Paint unifies. Paint protects. And paint has no peer when it comes to squeezing the most out of each dollar spent on remodeling. *** There's more to it than dipping your brush in a bucket, however. Painting techniques are much like paint itself: deceptively complicated. Doing the job right demands specific responses to a host of unpredictable and nearly imperceptible variables, from the ever-changing chemistry of paint itself to the moisture content and surface porosity of the surface. Add the vagaries of weather and you'll understand why a success in Seattle might flake in Sarasota. Get a guide if you aim to paint right. *** John Dee has wielded the brush (and scraper and roller and spray gun) for many of the projects *This Old House* has tackled. Like master carpenter Norm Abram, Dee is a craftsman who knows not only what works, but also why. In the following pages, drawn from *This Old House* magazine, Dee and other craftsmen will introduce you to the essentials.

—THE EDITORS

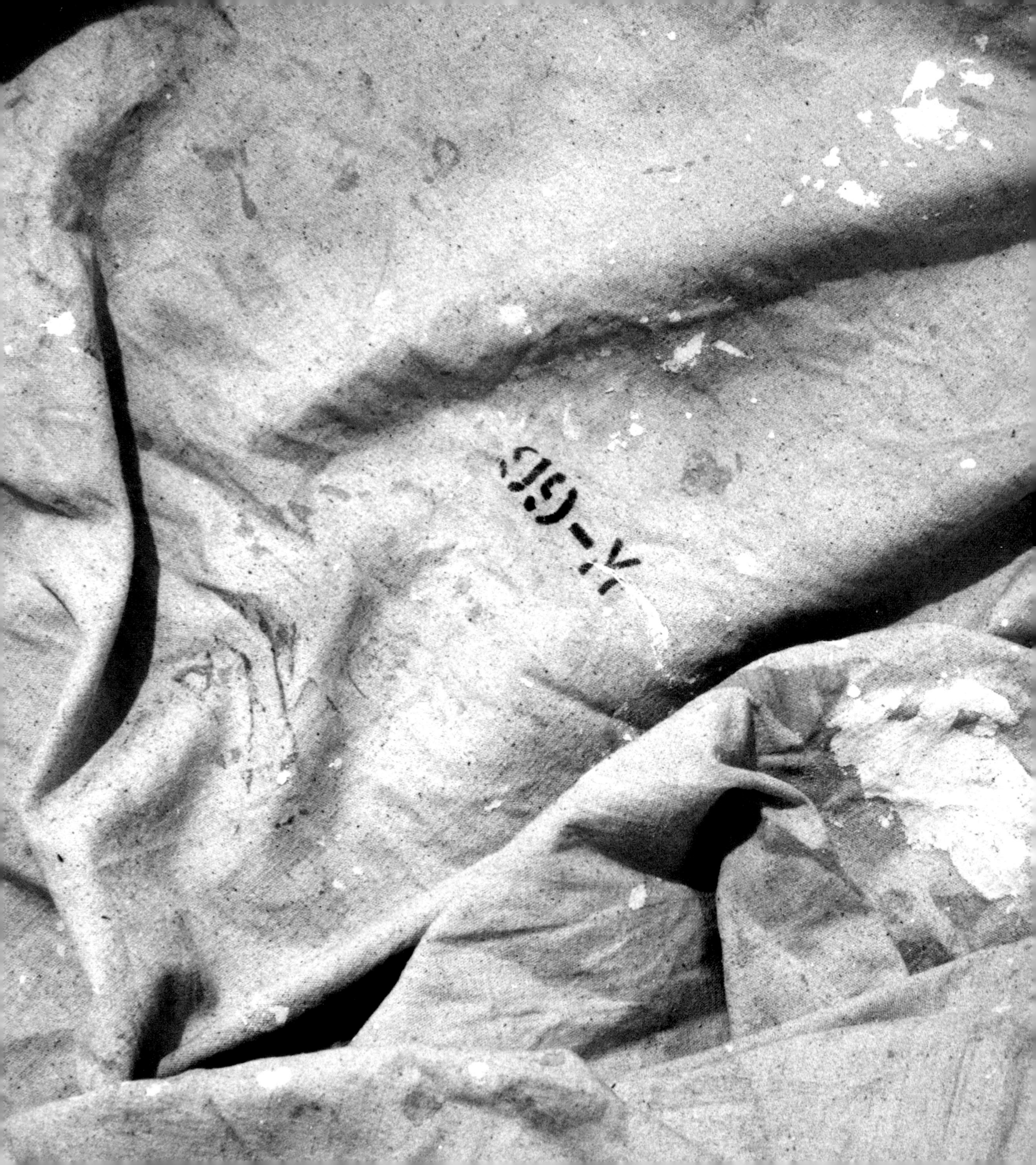

"LULLED BY THE SIMPLICITY OF THEIR TOOLS AND THE PENSIVE RHYTHM OF BRUSH STROKES, PAINTERS FREQUENTLY FALL OFF LADDERS, SEAR THEIR LUNGS and scour their SKIN."

[workingsafely]

PAINT HIDES MORE than you think. Beyond the glossy layer or the stylish masquerade of a faux finish is another deception: that painting is the safest home improvement. It is not. Lulled by the simplicity of their tools and the pensive rhythm of brush strokes, painters too frequently fall off ladders, sear their lungs and scour their skin. Take the work seriously: Gear up right.

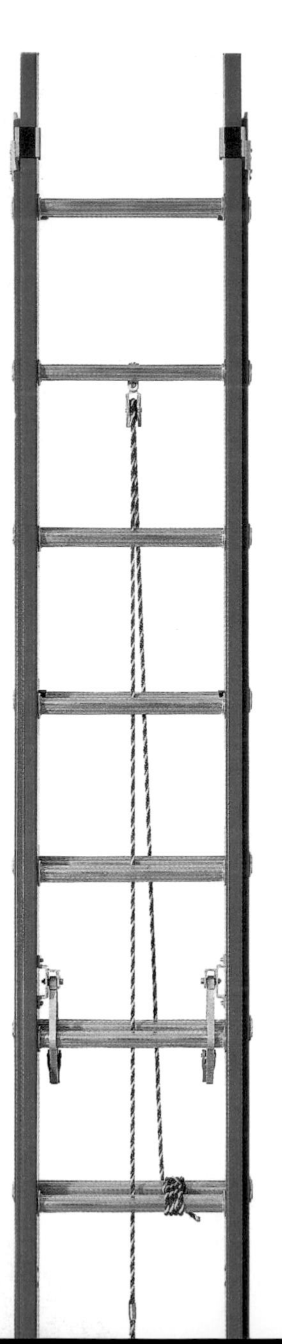

LADDERS

Professionals who spend their lives aloft know that when it comes to ladders, only one thing matters: They must remain stationary. And the first bit of advice is: Don't be cheap. "Buy the best you can," says Tom Silva. "Life's too valuable to cut costs." Tom uses only commercial- or industrial-grade aluminum ladders. But there are other options. Ladders come in three materials—wood, aluminum and fiberglass (left)—and four grades: light household duty; commercial (for painters and general handymen); industrial (for contractors and maintenance workers); and professional grade (for rugged industrial and construction use). The most important difference between the grades is the weight they will carry—from a 200-pound maximum for household-duty ladders to 300 pounds for professional grade. Aluminum ladders are durable, reasonably light and easy to care for, making them good for general construction duty. Fiberglass ladders are slightly heavier, but they're favored by electricians for their non-conductivity.

Having chosen a good ladder, there's the critical business of setting it up. According to John Dee, a painting contractor in Concord, Massachusetts, a ladder's feet should be planted away from the wall one-quarter of the ladder's extended length. Tom uses the L-shaped diagram stuck on each of the ladder's rails as his guide. If the L's short leg is horizontal and its long leg is plumb, the ladder is at the correct angle.

Once a ladder is at the proper angle, it needs solid footing to stay that way. On soft ground, turn pivoting shoes so they dig in or drive wooden stakes behind the shoes to prevent slippage. When the ground is too hard, tying off a lower rung to an immovable post or two is cheap insurance, Dee says. Even after a ladder is placed, staked and tied, Dee doesn't climb until he applies his cardinal rule: "Settle the issue of ladder stability on the first rung." Dee fixes any problem before climbing past that point. "Never stand a ladder on a drop cloth," he adds.

But common sense is the most important ingredient when working with ladders. "Reach with your arms, not your body" is Dee's

When Tom lifts or lowers an extension ladder, he keeps both hands on the rope, well away from the sliding rungs that could mangle his fingers.

[workingsafely]

indoors and up

EXTENSION LADDERS RULE FOR OUTDOOR HEIGHTS, BUT A STEPLADDER IS THE KING OF LOWER REACHES INDOORS. MADE OF THE SAME MATERIALS AS EXTENSION LADDERS AND TO THE SAME LOAD RATINGS, STEPLADDERS ARE LIGHTWEIGHT AND MANEUVERABLE. DON'T LET ITS LOWER HEIGHT LULL YOU INTO CARELESSNESS, HOWEVER, BECAUSE A FALL FROM EVEN A FEW FEET CAN BE CATASTROPHIC. NEVER CLIMB HIGHER THAN 2 FEET BELOW THE TOP OF A STEPLADDER, AND DON'T SIT ON ITS TOP—YOUR WEIGHT CAN EASILY EXERT ENOUGH LEVERAGE TO TIP THE LADDER. TEMPTING AS IT MIGHT BE, DON'T CLIMB A CLOSED STEPLADDER, EITHER, EVEN IF IT SEEMS TO BE RESTING SECURELY AGAINST A WALL; IF IT'S ANGLED STEEPLY ENOUGH TO KEEP YOU FROM TIPPING BACKWARD, IT'S ALSO ANGLED ENOUGH FOR THE FEET TO SLIP OUT FROM UNDER YOU.

advice. He's seen people carrying fully extended ladders and walking backwards—blind to limbs, windows and power lines. "Always collapse an extension ladder before moving it," Tom says.

RESPIRATORS

After experiencing allergic reactions to latex paint, Steve Thomas wears a respirator whenever he paints. It's not a flimsy dust mask but rather a silicone half-face respirator that accepts organic-vapor cartridges for protection against fumes from latex paint and solvents. A common nuisance-dust mask sifts out small particles of dust, but it's no defense against fumes. Respirators rely on replaceable cartridges to sift out the harmful elements in gases and vapors. Cartridges work only for specific contaminants, however, and they wear out, sometimes even when not in use. If you smell what you're using or feel dizzy, get fresh air and replace the cartridges. If the problem recurs quickly, the mask doesn't suit the work.

A quality silicone rubber mask will maximize your comfort, but it's not a respirator unless it has a label from NIOSH, the National Institute for Occupational Safety and Health. But even the best respirator won't work if facial hair breaks the seal—anyone with a beard may need more exotic gear.

But good as respirators are, it's always a good idea to implement some other safety precautions as well. When painting indoors, open a window and set a fan in an opposite doorway, blowing toward you. Stand in the stream of fresh air. Be especially cautious if you have chronic health problems or are painting in close quarters.

GLOVES AND BOOTS

A good glove is expensive but costs far less than a skin graft. Paint chemicals are hard on skin, so take time to choose a glove carefully.

Latex, a natural rubber, makes great dishwashing gloves but offers little protection against strong chemicals. Nitrile and neoprene, synthetic rubbers, are more puncture-resistant than latex and resist mineral-spirit solvents (but not acetone). Butyl, also a synthetic rubber, is better for solvents such as acetone and ketones. PVC, a plastic, is good for acids, caustics, cleaning materials and most alcohols.

Polyethylene gloves are cheap but they tear easily and won't resist most dangerous chemicals. PVA-coated gloves are excellent for organic compounds, methylene chloride (used in many strippers) and chlorinated solvents such as the ones in degreasers. Water dissolves the coating, however, so don't use them in water or water-based solutions.

Tom says this of boots: "Think of boots as tools." The right pair makes any job easier. But when you're up a ladder, slip-resistance is the feature you'll appreciate the most.

Safety gear. 1. PVA-coated gloves (top) will stand up to paint strippers. Polyethylene gloves (bottom) keep hands clean while stirring paint, but don't protect. 2. A scaffold mounted on locking wheels brings tall ceilings within reach while saving ladder-climbing time. Collapsible models are the most portable. 3. A half-face respirator, shown here, guards against toxic fumes though it doesn't protect eyes from chemical and solvent splashes. 4. A conventional square heel, rather than a wedge heel, keeps feet from slipping off ladder rungs. Soles made of nitrile, a durable synthetic rubber, reduce slippage as well.

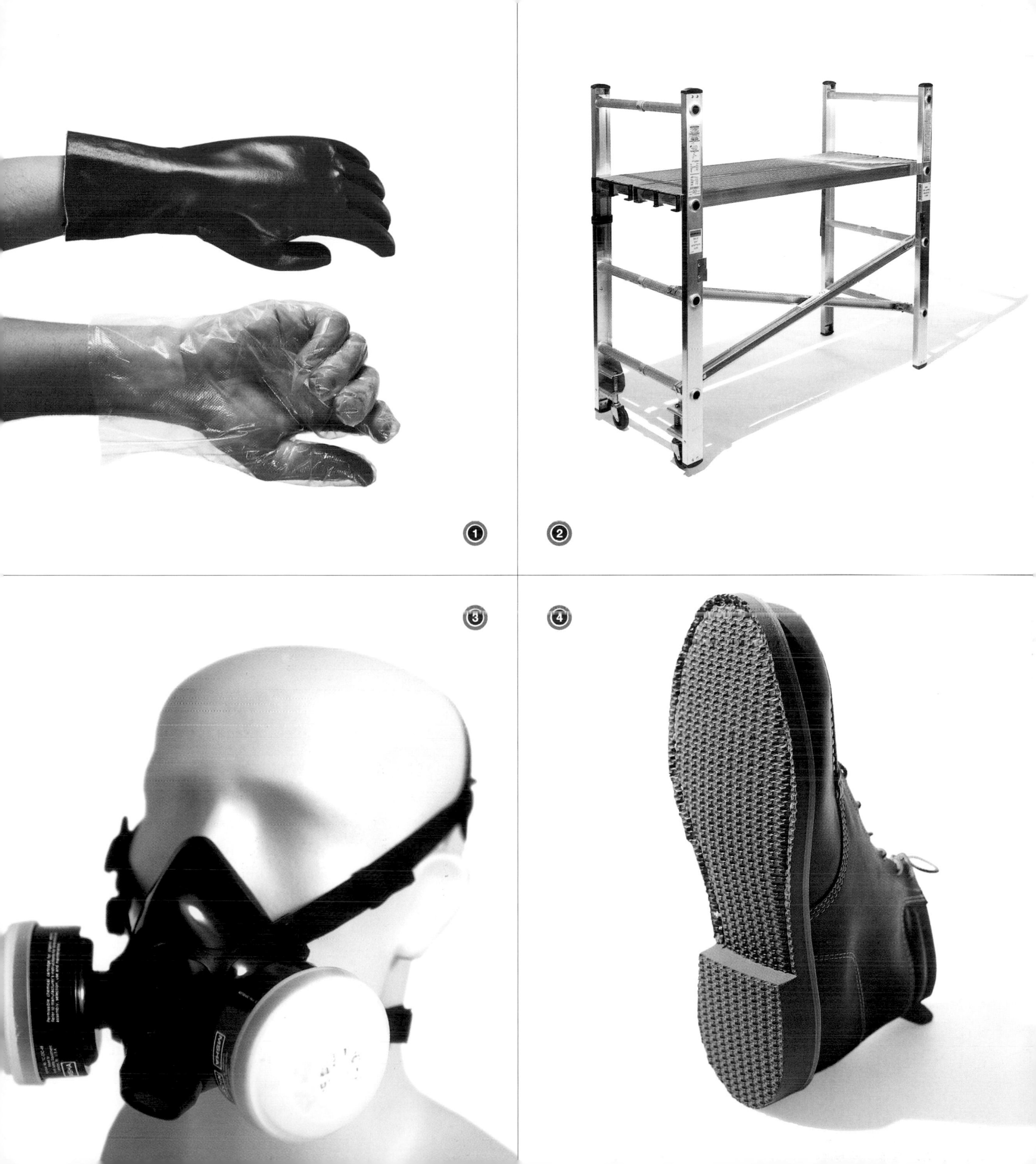
1
2
3
4

[paintpreptools]

ASK PAINTERS FOR A one-word synopsis of how to paint and you'll get one answer more than any other: "Prepare." In fact, painting is a craft that rewards those best who prepare the most, and there's more to it than slathering on primer. If a surface isn't sound and clean, even the finest painter using the best brush loaded with expensive paint will get mediocre results. A few carefully chosen tools can make short work of this unpleasant job. Paint scrapers (see page 98) are one option, and they can claw off loose paint all day.

Fitted with a stiff blade instead of a sanding pad, this detail sander can scrape paint from metal.

But when sound paint is the surface that must be removed—or roughed up—to prepare for subsequent paint coats, the job usually ends up in the hands of power sanders, siding strippers or hand scrapers.

DETAIL SANDERS

If you have ever sanded the paint-clogged crevices of a double-hung window, you've surely developed an intense dislike for sanding blocks: The makeshift tool is simple but agonizingly slow. Next time, try a detail sander, a svelte power sander that looks like a platypus and hums like barber's clippers. Often called a corner sander (for the tight spots it reaches) or a triangle sander (for its distinctive pad), the points of a detail sander's triangular pad slip easily into corners and slide along edges. With his detail sanders, Tom Silva can smooth every nuance of a staircase newel, then slip between balusters to sand steps. "They're also great," he says, "for sanding window trim and touching up the corners of windowsills." There are three types of detail sanders.

Oscillating detail sanders have a triangular sanding pad mounted on a spindle that jitters back and forth. If the spindle is attached to the side of the sanding pad, the whole pad pivots back and forth like a high-speed windshield wiper; if it's attached at the center, the pad moves with a twisting motion. Tom arms his sanders with fuzzy-backed hook-and-loop papers that can be pulled off and repositioned in an instant when one tip loses grit. Oscillating sanders inevitably sand across wood grain, although the minuscule distance traveled by the pad (barely 1/16 inch at the tips) minimizes scratching.

Orbital detail sanders look just like their oscillating cousins, but the pad orbits in tight circles, an action less likely to leave cross-grain scratches.

In-line detail sanders, instead of oscillating or orbiting, move forward and back at speeds that would burn calluses off the hardiest hand-sander. At the business end of each in-line sander is a hollow or solid rubber "profile" that gives the sandpaper its surface-hugging

The ferret-like detail sander noses into places other power sanders can't reach, eliminating the need for tedious sanding by hand. It won't kick up much dust, either.

[paintpreptools]

shape. These tools are best at smoothing long, curved surfaces such as traditional stair spindles, or working along milled profiles such as baseboard and similar moldings.

RANDOM ORBIT SANDERS

You'll probably cringe the first time you sweep a random-orbit sander across the grain of a tabletop. But as the surface begins to smooth with no sign of scratching, you'll see that, unlike other sanders, this tool works equally well running with the grain or across it.

A random-orbit sander incorporates two simultaneous actions: As the pad spins in circles, it also moves in an elliptical orbit. The motion isn't truly random, but the two motions overlap as you work, reducing scratching across the grain and keeping any swirl marks to a minimum. The eccentric movement of the sanding pad lets you disregard grain direction entirely, a real time-saver on furniture and cabinet projects.

Versatility is another random-orbit hallmark. The tool can strip paint like a belt sander but is easier to control. It can finish like an orbital sander but without provoking grain-direction worries. And because it can suck up and remove dust through holes in the pad, a random-orbit sander is great where ventilation is lousy or when dust must be minimized. "This tool," says Norm, "is starting to dominate my sander collection."

Using the right sandpaper is crucial if a

Random-Orbit Sanders: 1. Sanding dust is sucked through holes in the sander's pad, but dust collection suffers if the holes in the pad don't line up with those in the sanding disc. Discs can have as few as five holes or as many as 16, so make sure the ones you buy match your machine. 2. A random-orbit sander can generate extremely fine dust, as Norm found when using his to sand this solid-surface countertop. He always connects his sander to a vacuum. 3. A random-orbit sander smoothes a wood surface no matter which way the grain is running, making it invaluable for sanding these pegged cabinet doors.

Belt Sanders: 1. The rotating dust bag of Tom's belt sander swings out of the way as he smooths stacks of shelving. He's making overlapping passes at an angle to the wood grain in order to remove stock quickly; later he'll remove cross-grain scratches by sanding with the grain. 2. Stripping paint brings out the best in a belt sander and the worst in belts. Tom keeps his sander moving constantly so as not to overheat the surface and clog the belt. Old paint may harbor lead, so he dons a respirator and connects the tool to a vacuum hose. 3. Paint buildup can be removed with a crepe rubber block held against a moving belt.

random-orbit sander is to deliver the best performance. Uncoated aluminum oxide is the best abrasive for raw wood. On painted or sealed wood, use stearated aluminum oxide discs to minimize clogging. "I start with 80 grit to strip a finish on solid wood,"says Norm, "otherwise the first step is 100 or 120 followed by 150. I stop there if the surface will be painted. If I'm staining, I go to 180 grit and then 220."

Palm-grip models with 5-inch pads are the lightweights of the random-orbit family (and they're usually the least expensive). They're easy to hold against narrow surfaces, such as cabinet face frames, and very maneuverable. Right-angle random-orbit sanders have gears that link a powerful motor to the sanding pad. You can push the tool hard without slowing it down—a plus if you're stripping paint. With a lighter touch and fine sandpaper, it also makes a great finish sander. An in-line random-orbit sander, with its motor directly over the pad, is mechanically identical to a palm-grip sander. In-lines, however, have stronger motors, variable-speed control and handles.

BELT SANDERS

Belt sanders are the chain saws of sanding machines: loud, aggressive and built to remove anything in a hurry, including paint. They are simple brutes, with a trigger switch, a motor, a dust bag and two rollers to guide the revolving sanding belt over a flat base plate. The motor drives the rear roller; the front roller is a lever-tensioned pulley that keeps the belt taut.

Belt size is the most important feature

[paintpreptools]

distinguishing one sander from another. The biggest use belts 4 inches wide and 24 inches in circumference, but you'll also find diminutive 3-by-18 models, as well as a few specialty sanders with belts barely an inch wide. Tom prefers the big sanders that can rip through decades of paint, grind off nail heads or level wide swaths of wood. These muscle machines are heavy—some tip the scales at up to 15 pounds—but Tom can usually flop work across a couple of sawhorses. Norm prefers a smaller belt sander for its maneuverability. "When you're trying to sand door casings without taking them off the jambs," he says, "a 3-by-21 is nice." Some models weigh less than six pounds.

Belt sanders are dust-generators almost without peer. A decent dust bag is essential, but it can choke trying to keep up with super-coarse belts. Tom hooks his sander to a shop vac whenever possible. He finds that vacuum-assisted belts clog less, so they're able to cut faster; they also throw less sawdust into the air. And when sanding any surface that might conceal a layer of lead-based paint, a vacuum (and a good respirator—see page 10) can keep toxic dust from invading your lungs.

A sanding belt's work is done by legions of tiny, chisel-sharp abrasive granules, or grit, graded by size from super-coarse 24 grit to silky 320. Closed-coat belts pack the grit tightly; they're best for sanding metal and hardwoods. Open-coat belts space out the grit to reduce clogging, so they work better on soft, pitchy woods like pine and for stripping paint. Aluminum-oxide grit, typically the least expensive, is good for general-duty wood sanding. All belts once had lumpy glued-and-lapped joints that would self-destruct unless turned in the proper direction (arrows inside the belt show which way they're supposed to rotate). Newer bidirectional belts have lump-free, taped joints that can be run in either direction. They also last 10 to 15 percent longer and tend to sand more smoothly than old-style belts.

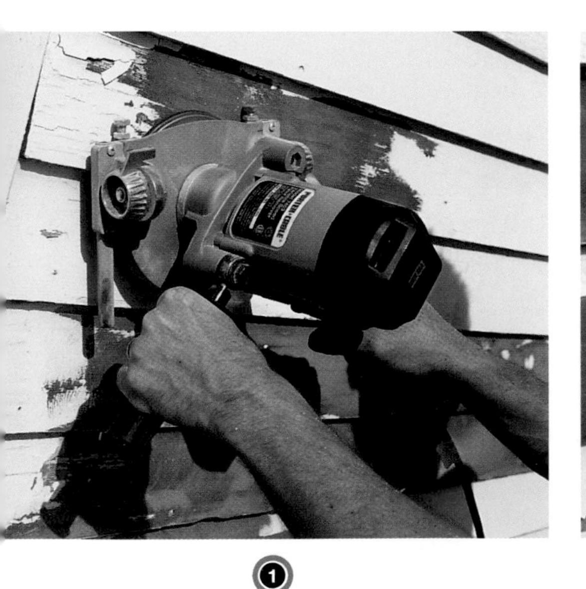

1 2

Power Siding-Strippers: 1. The upright style of this stripper can be tricky to balance, but auxiliary handles help. 2. The barrel-grip configuration of this model is easier to balance but may be difficult for small hands to hold for long periods. Either tool takes practice to use properly. Wear safety glasses to protect against flying shards of paint.

POWER SIDING-STRIPPERS

Sanding or hand-scraping the paint from wood siding is hardly a job you take on for fun. Next time you face such a dreary prospect, consider a specialty tool that's often called a power siding-stripper. One version has an acrylic dust shroud with a vacuum port that captures the paint planed off by three spinning carbide "teeth." If lead might be in the paint you're removing, however, equip your face with a respirator and your vacuum with a HEPA filter (a high-efficiency filter). Another power stripper whirls a 6-inch tungsten/carbide-studded disk at 3,500 to 4,500 rpm, abrading everything in its path. Use it only on lead-free paint, though, because it flings lots of dust. Neither tool can reach into corners, and both may leave swirls that require sanding, but either one will save lots of scraping. Don't forget to set any nails before you begin.

Hand Scrapers: 1. A gooseneck scraper is shaped like a draftsman's French curve. Sprung between fingers and thumb, it fits the shape of many moldings. 2. Some contractors figure that stripping paint with a hand scraper is safer than using a toxic liquid stripper. Wetting the surface before hand scraping keeps down dust.

HAND SCRAPERS

A hand scraper is the simplest of tools—just a thin piece of steel with a hooked edge. But that tiny hook, drawn across wood, can shave a rough surface smooth in less time than a razor can clear-cut days of beard from a cheek. Before the invention of sandpaper in the late 19th century, wood was often smoothed with scrapers or hand planes. A finely tuned hand scraper cuts cleaner than sandpaper anyway, because it shears the wood. Sandpaper scours wood, leaving behind a surface that looks smooth but may feel fuzzy.

Scrapers cannot be used indiscriminately, however. On the bare surface of pine and other softwoods, scraping may crush fibers or rip them from the surface, leaving pits. But scrapers work quite well on most hardwoods, even on highly figured boards such as bird's-eye maple, and the tool makes such a shallow cut that there's little danger of tearing fibers, regardless of which direction they face.

Curved scrapers can be used instead of detail sanders to remove paint from complex moldings. For final passes on fine work, the barely visible hook on the scraper's edge works well, but for rough work, such as removing old paint, the edge can be used without elaboration. A scraper can slice off brushstrokes before a final coat of paint is applied and pare off gummy masking-tape residue. Think of it as a device for removing bits of anything, and there's no limit to what a hand scraper can do.

[caulking joints]

CAULK PERFORMS ONE basic task: It fills gaps. Our needs for it are almost as simple: to seal things in or keep them out (water, hot air, cold air, insects...even fire), or to beautify, as when we cover the inevitable fissure between straight trim and wavy walls. But this seemingly modest material is a compex brew of ingredients designed to shut up and stay put, and using the right caulk in the right place for the right reasons is one hallmark of paint craftsmanship. Using it to cover up sloppy carpentry is not what the stuff is for.

with practice, *you'll be amazed at how neat a bead you can lay straight from a caulking gun. The goal is to tuck the bead into a joint with one pass (or less) of your little finger, with no excess to wipe off.*

Until the 1950s, the composition of most caulk was as straightforward as its purpose. Often called putty, it was usually made of ground limestone (calcium carbonate) and a drying oil such as soybean, tung or linseed. But putty hardened, and it cracked when joint walls moved. This limitation inspired the development of today's array of elastomeric caulks, which stretch and compress—sometimes even as much as their manufacturers claim. While the terms caulk and sealant are often used interchangeably, caulk generally refers to compounds with low elasticity. Sealants stretch and compress better, cost more and last longer.

Caulk and sealant chemists constantly fiddle with chemical recipes so their products will perform in a particular way. Binders, such as silicone and latex, have the greatest effect on the product's flexibility, durability and adhesion. Fillers control consistency. Additives run the gamut from colorants to mildewcides. Liquids—either water or solvents—hold the ingredients together in suspension. Whatever the mix, it doesn't pay to be cheap when buying a caulk or sealant. A new home or major renovation might consume four 12-tube cases, but even on a really big job, "you're talking about $150 for caulk," says Mark Fitzpatrick, project manager for *This Old House*'s renovation in Savannah, Georgia. Trying to shave $50 by switching to a low-end sealant will cost more in the long run. Good contractors typically choose caulks and sealants based on extensive personal experimentation. Fitzpatrick favors polyurethane for exterior applications because it's durable, easily painted and adheres tenaciously. Painting contractor John Dee waxes eloquent on the crack-hiding qualities of siliconized acrylic latex for interior trim. Take a peek at what Tom Silva loads in his caulk gun and you'll often find the same thing.

Until about 12 years ago, silicone and latex were the only high-quality choices. But manufacturers have since cooked up hundreds of recipes for specific tasks, from patching aluminum gutters

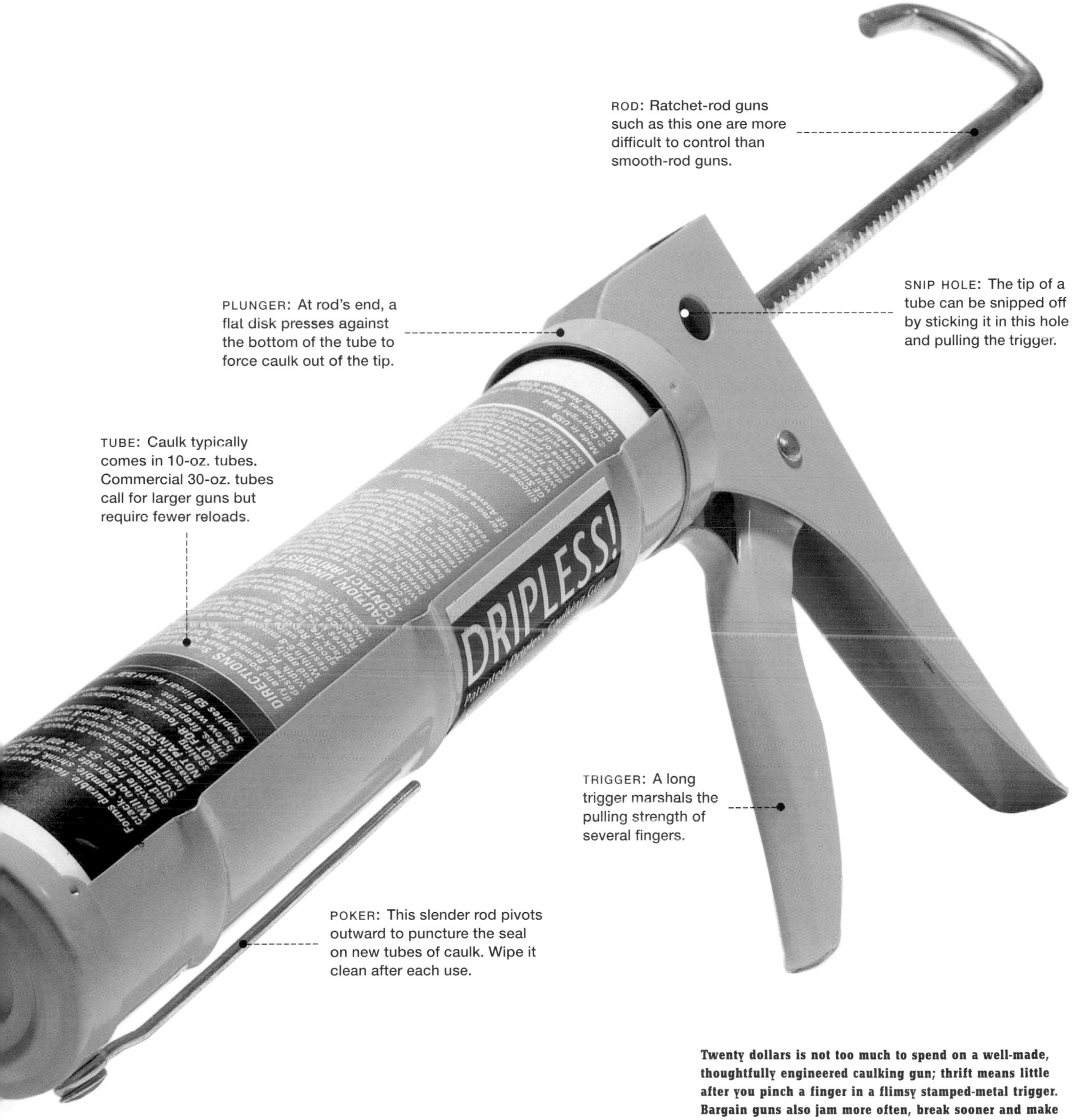

ROD: Ratchet-rod guns such as this one are more difficult to control than smooth-rod guns.

PLUNGER: At rod's end, a flat disk presses against the bottom of the tube to force caulk out of the tip.

SNIP HOLE: The tip of a tube can be snipped off by sticking it in this hole and pulling the trigger.

TUBE: Caulk typically comes in 10-oz. tubes. Commercial 30-oz. tubes call for larger guns but require fewer reloads.

TRIGGER: A long trigger marshals the pulling strength of several fingers.

POKER: This slender rod pivots outward to puncture the seal on new tubes of caulk. Wipe it clean after each use.

Twenty dollars is not too much to spend on a well-made, thoughtfully engineered caulking gun; thrift means little after you pinch a finger in a flimsy stamped-metal trigger. Bargain guns also jam more often, break sooner and make a painter's life miserable. But loaded with high-quality paintable caulk, a good gun is an invaluable sidekick.

[caulkingjoints]

to filling cracks in asphalt or repairing glass aquariums. Sometimes the same ingredients show up with labels specifying different uses. That's just plain old target marketing. (A tip: Silicones marked "for marine use" are often no different from everyday household silicones but cost twice as much.) Or the same sealant can be tested to different specifications. Or the variation in two formulas is so slight that the ingredients listed on the labels appear to be the same. And because manufacturers are responsible for testing their own products, label claims should be regarded with healthy skepticism.

Even the best caulk will fail if not applied correctly. Surfaces must be dry and scrupulously clean—free of dirt, oils and flaking paint. Give joints a thorough scrubbing with a solvent such as rubbing alcohol. Old caulk can sometimes be loosened with a heat gun. Before caulking, Dee always brushes primer on raw wood to promote adhesion. And beware: A sealant applied too deeply into a joint will stretch poorly and is likely to fail. Even shallow joints will fail if sealant adheres to both joint walls and substrate (bond-breaker tape applied to the bottom of such joints solves the problem).

After application, a bead of sealant should be tooled into the joint. This fills voids, promotes adhesion and produces a clean look. A plastic spoon or wooden tongue depressor gives more consistent results than a moistened finger. Sealants that skin over quickly, such as silicone, should be tooled immediately. Proper application matters because virtually all warranties cover only the sealant. If a leak causes $10,000 in damage, all you'll get back is the $3 you paid for the tube. But no matter how advanced sealants become, says Norm Abram, they'll never take the place of good design and careful carpentry. "We see a lot of places where someone has used sealant to make up for poor workmanship," he says. "No sealant is foolproof. You want a design that sheds water naturally. Good workmanship will last a lot longer than any sealant."

« "No matter how chemically advanced sealants become," says Norm, "they'll never take the place of good design and careful carpentry." »

Sealant depth should be no more than half its width; in deep joints, press a polyurethane foam backer rod (left) into the joint before applying the sealant. The rod also prevents sealant from adhering to more than two surfaces of the joint. Various caulks (right) accept paint well.

POLYURETHANE
Flexibility: ±25%
Shrinkage: <5%
Adhesion: excellent
Service Life: 15 years if painted or protected from sun
UV resistance: low (white lasts longest)
Best uses: any joint subject to abrasion, such as a driveway seam

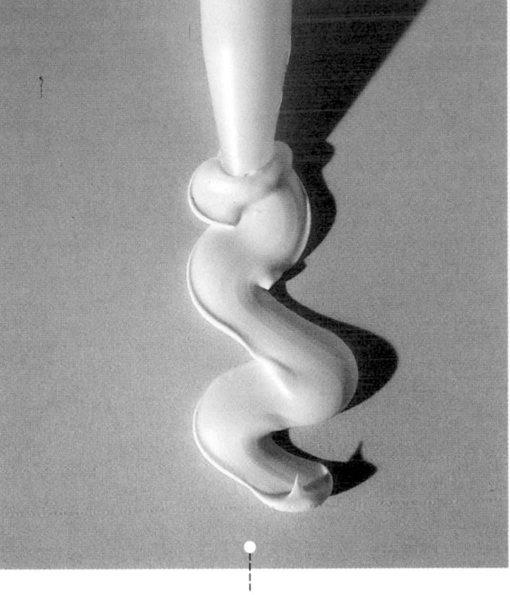

LATEX
Flexibility: ±5%
Shrinkage: 10% to 20%
Adhesion: fair
Service Life: 5 to 10 years
UV resistance: fair
Best uses: low-movement interior joints

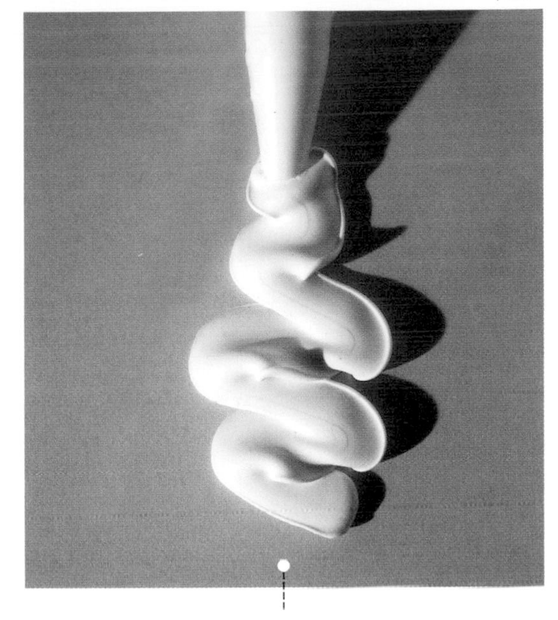

SILICONIZED ACRYLIC LATEX
Flexibility:±10% to 20%
Shrinkage: 20%
Adhesion: good
Service Life: indoors, 20 years; outdoors, 10 to 15 years in low-stress situations
UV resistance: good
Best uses: interior, paintable surfaces

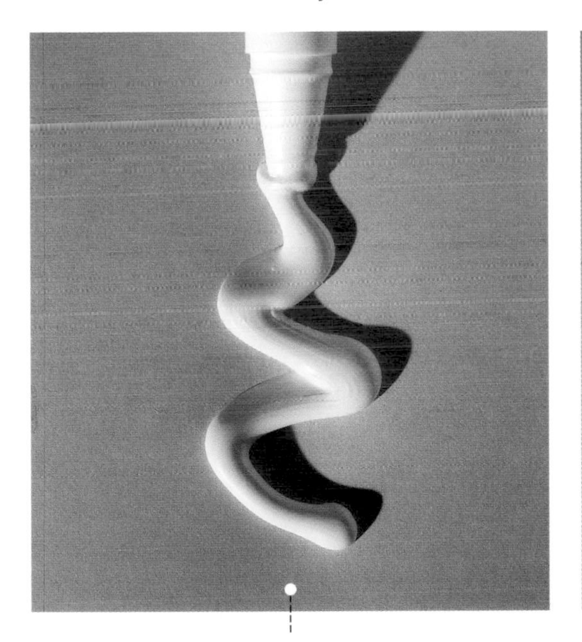

SILICONE LATEX
Flexibility: ±25%
Shrinkage: 10%
Adhesion: excellent
Service Life: 15 years
UV resistance: excellent
Best uses: for general purposes, indoors and out

POLYSULFIDE
Flexibility: ±25%
Shrinkage: <5%
Adhesion: good
Service Life: 15 years if protected from sun
UV resistance: poor
Best uses: outdoors, in situations where there is moderate movement

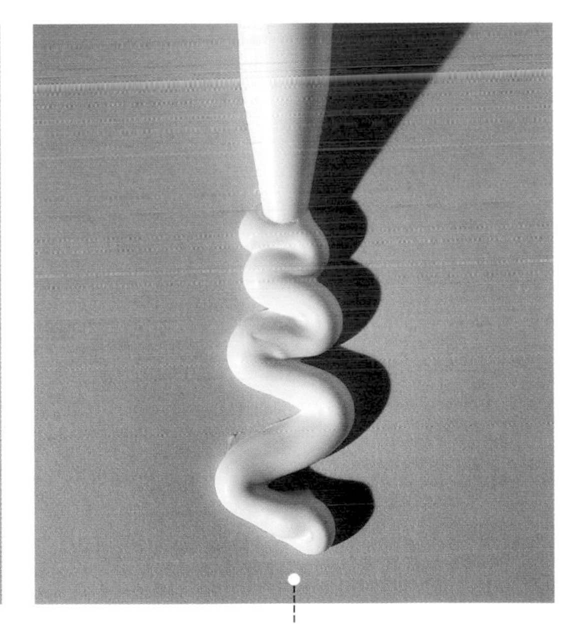

ACRYLIC LATEX
Flexibility: ±10% to ±20%
Shrinkage: clear, 20%; pigmented, 10%
Adhesion: good to porous surfaces, poor to nonporous ones
Service life: 20 yrs. inside; 10-15 yrs. outside
UV resistance: good
Best uses: patching interior cracks, joints and small holes prior to painting

[caulkingjoints]

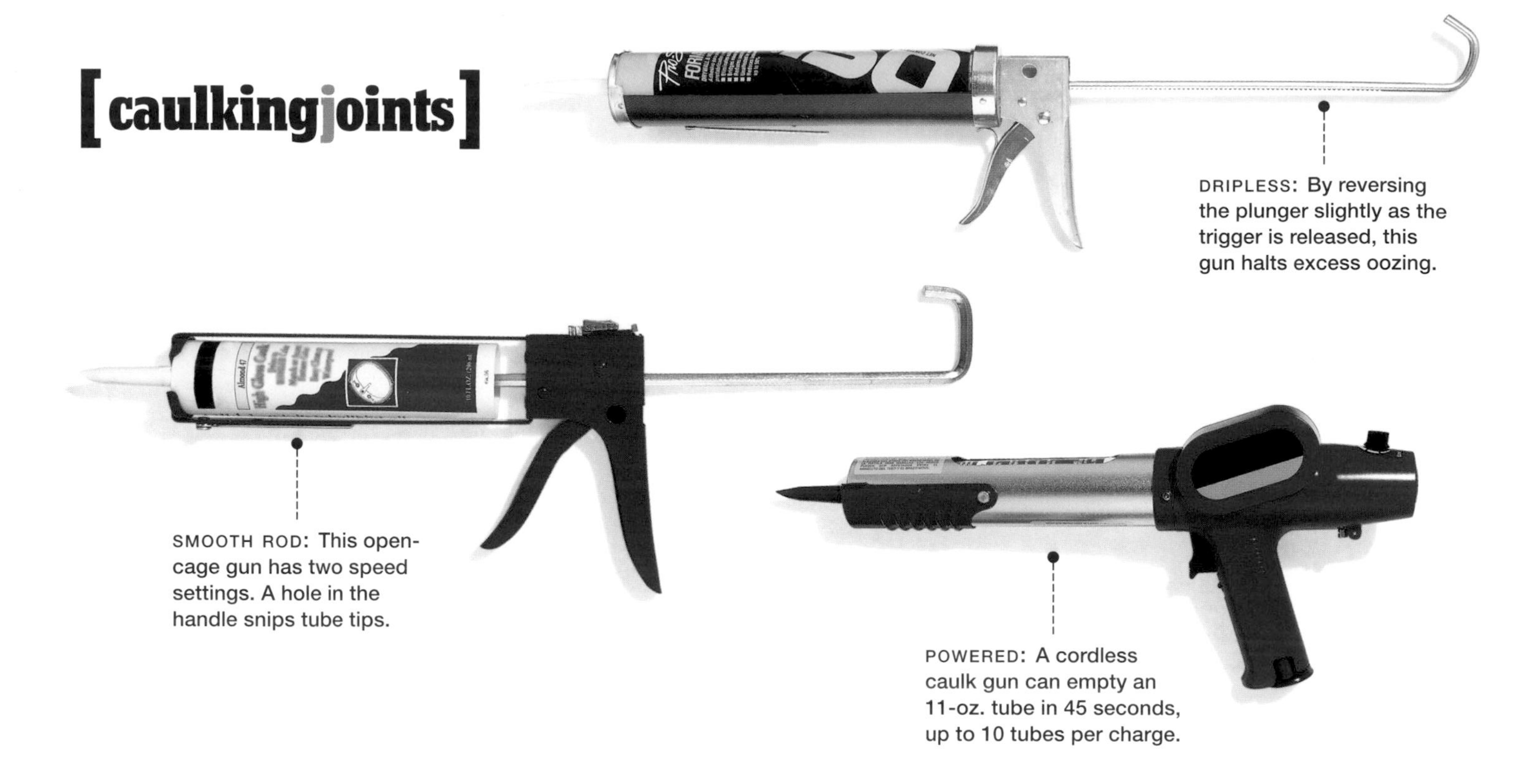

DRIPLESS: By reversing the plunger slightly as the trigger is released, this gun halts excess oozing.

SMOOTH ROD: This open-cage gun has two speed settings. A hole in the handle snips tube tips.

POWERED: A cordless caulk gun can empty an 11-oz. tube in 45 seconds, up to 10 tubes per charge.

* * *

CAULKING GUNS

OF ALL THE CONSTRUCTION TOOLS EVER INVENTED, THE INEXPENSIVE ratchet-rod caulking gun just might be the most difficult to control. Squeezing the trigger advances the piston, causing fiendishly sticky stuff to burp forth.

Mere humans must move the gun's opaque tip in perfect synchronicity with each gush of goo. Caulk masters leave a smooth, slightly rounded bead in the gun's wake, not the "squirrel-ribby" row of ridges or other hesitation marks that would make it look more like knotted clothesline than a taut white cord. The trick these guys know sounds simple: Maintain an even pressure against the joint, keeping the tip in motion as long as sealant oozes out. But as any student driver will tell you, it's not driving that's so hard—it's all the starting and stopping. When an expert caulker finishes a joint, he snaps the bead with a gentle downward twist, quickly disengages the piston rod and covers the tip of the cartridge with his thumb. Even the explosive pop of an air bubble won't faze him. He just backtracks an inch and pulls the bead flat again, plowing right through the blotched ejecta. Then, with a damp rag and a putty knife,

caulking tip

CAULK, APPLIED SPARINGLY TO JOINTS, IS THE SECRET OF A SEAMLESS PAINT JOB. PAINTING CONTRACTOR JOHN DEE HAS A TECHNIQUE FOR CUTTING THE TIP OF A CAULK TUBE THAT MINIMIZES WASTE AND, INSTEAD OF DEPOSITING THE CAULK IN BLOBS, MAKES A CRISP CORNER. FIRST, HE CUTS A 45-DEGREE ANGLE AS CLOSE AS POSSIBLE TO THE TUBE'S TIP, THEN HE SANDS THE OPENING WITH 120-GRIT SANDPAPER GLUED TO THE INSIDE OF A SMALL PIECE OF CORNER MOLDING. THIS CREATES A TIP THAT CAN BE PUSHED TIGHT AGAINST THE JOINT. JUST DON'T FORGET TO USE PAINTABLE CAULK.

he deftly cleans up the splattered caulk on both sides of the hiccup. Painters love to follow this kind of workmanship. And does the craftsman caulker ever wet a finger and run it down his bead? No, this trick reeks of apology: "Having messed up the bead of caulk, I hereby make a sorry attempt to smear it uniformly, leaving this thumb-fatted bead for the painter to hide."

The first caulking gun appears to have been invented in 1894 as a "puttying tool," but it's possible they were first used in bakeries to apply icing. The gun didn't gain widespread acceptance as a device for caulking until the early '60s, when disposable cartridges made their appearance. Before World War II, even such things as bathtubs were commonly sealed using a putty knife.

Some contractors prefer an open-cage caulking gun (the so-called skeleton strap) for the small caulk tubes, so they can turn the entire tube to adjust the angle of tip contact. Larger guns often employ the heavier open-barrel design, solid as a safe and irresistible as a nutcracker. They're often loaded with tubes of glue and mastic, which by their nature require more thrust to dispense than painter's caulk. Good guns have either smooth-rods or hex-rods that respond to delicate pressure on the trigger, allowing more control of the amount of sealant dispensed than the clicking ratchet-rod models do. The best caulking guns have some kind of trigger or thumb-lever to release piston pressure at joint's end. Without that, caulk will continue to leak from the tip.

But perhaps the greatest caulking debate deals less with the gun than with how it's used. Many contractors pull the gun as caulk is dispensed, partly because the bead is always visible and there's no danger of brushing against it with an elbow. Those who push, however, insist that pushing the tip not only forces the bead flat but is also easier because the pushing motion eliminates minor hesitations caused by arm tremors. And pushing can be done with one hand, while good pulling requires two: one on the barrel and one on the trigger. Try both ways and see which one works best for you.

[paintbrushes]

Most paint pros can extract an arsenal

of modern painting tools from the back

OF THEIR TRUCK, INCLUDING VARIEGATED DROPCLOTHS, PAINT-splattered ladders and vines of hoses for exotic spray gear. But in tight spots, when cutting in along walls and ceilings or finishing surfaces such as cabinets and trim, one simple tool is the unchallenged favorite: a paintbrush. That's because brush work is efficient. Cleanup is fast. And control—with a little practice—can be as precise as calligraphy.

Save old brushes:
A good paintbrush rarely wears out; it's more likely to die of neglect. If you've invested in good brushes, however, all is not lost if you accidentally forget to clean one. Special brush solvents are available to resurrect even those caked with modern coatings such as polyurethane. Check at a paint store; these products are fairly new.

[paintbrushes]

Without the cacophony of rattling compressors, a brush lets a painter work in tranquillity. Painters learn early to identify the good ones, and to realize that they're like any other fine tool—costly: Do-it-yourselfers accustomed to buying "throw-aways" are often aghast at the cost of fine brushes, not realizing that they can last for decades if properly cleaned and stored.

a cheap brush, *says John Dee, "sheds like a dog." It's also hard to control, can't cut a clean line and has a tendency to drip when going between can and surface.*

The best ones have bristles packed, glued and bound to handles so securely that it's easier to pull a hair from your head than pluck one from the brush. The others? "They can be uncomfortable—poorly balanced—and just won't hold up to cleaning," says Dee.

When the pros look for a good brush, the process is often more tactile than visual. Standing at a rack full of new brushes, they remove the stiff keeper protecting the bristles and make a close inspection. The business end gets a firm tug to see how well anchored the bristles are. Then they push, stroke and fan the brush against the back of a hand or a chin, feeling for the softness that indicates supple, extensively flagged tips (the brush equivalent of split ends). Like a legion of tiny feather dusters, these tips help smooth brush marks as well as push paint into a surface's microscopic crevices. Many painters believe a brush still does this better than anything. Dee, for one, insists on brushing siding seconds after he spray-paints it in order to work in the finish.

The construction of a brush determines whether it carries paint to a wall for hours with dripless legerdemain or needs frequent stops for reloading. Most ferrules are not packed solid with hair or filament. Spread them and you'll see a spacer plug, which creates a reservoir that fills with paint as the brush is dipped in the can. As the brush is stroked across a surface, paint squeezes along tapered filaments to be dispersed by the flagged tips. The void also lets solvent penetrate into the ferrule area during cleaning. Brushes without spacers, such as the finest European brushes for oil-based paints, work as well, say some; the extra bristles lift more paint from the can. Dee uses both kinds but says solid-packed brushes are harder to clean.

Thorough and frequent cleaning—and matching the brush to the paint—are the keys to this long-lived tool. A professional painter won't hesitate to stop for the few minutes it takes to clean a brush that feels saturated and unresponsive or that has paint drying in the filaments near the ferrule. Animal-hair brushes are best used in oil-based (alkyd) finishes: Water makes them too floppy. Nylon and polyester brushes can be used in either paint, but avoid going back and forth between the two with the same brush. "There are solvents in latex paint that react with the oils in alkyds and leave a gummy mess in the ferrule," says Dee. "Once it happens, the brush is ruined." Dee marks brush handles to distinguish them: red for oil, blue for latex.

Even with the best care, any brush will eventually falter. Painter Pat Chism reaches for just such a brush to flick dust off the top of door trim. "It started off painting like any other," he says. "Now it's my duster. There's always some life left in a good brush."

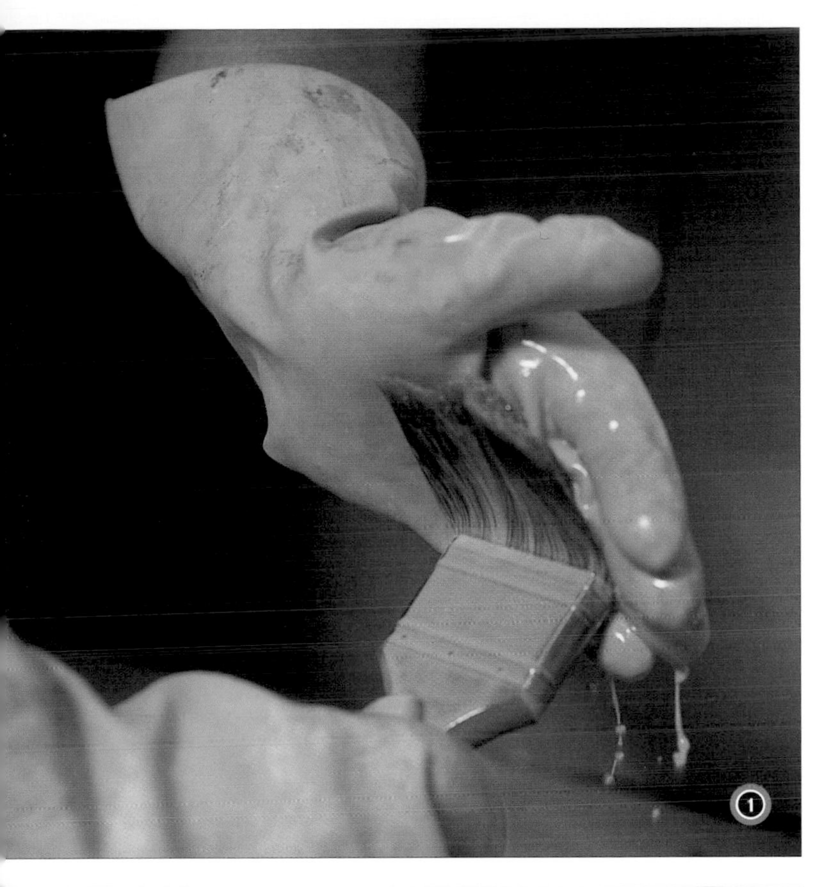

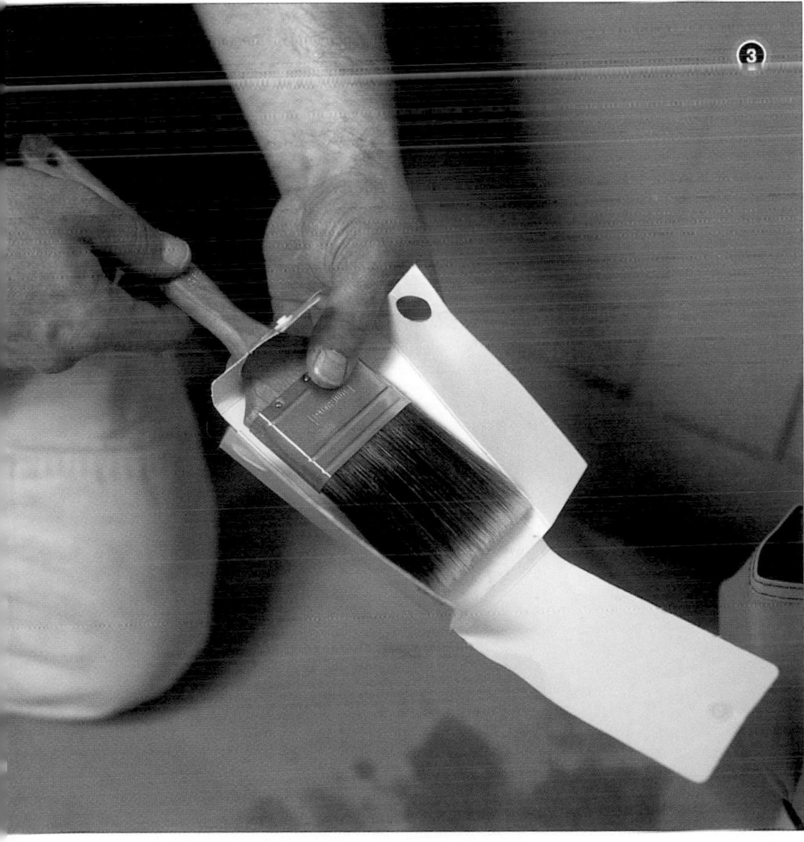

TECHNIQUES

Thin: A good, expensive brush deserves to be cleaned well and often. When cleaning brushes used with oil paints, wear rubber gloves to protect your hands and work in a well-ventilated area to defend your lungs against accumulating solvent fumes. Vigorously force thinner into the bristles (1), then tip the brush up so that solvent will seep well down into the ferrule. When cleaning brushes used in latex paints, use clean water and dish soap instead of solvent, otherwise follow much the same cleaning process.

Rinse: Solvent left in the bristles can foul your next brush-full of paint, so take pains to remove any residue. Rinse the brush four times (save the thinner in a sealed container for reuse; solids will eventually settle in the bottom). After each rinse, spin the brush dry (2) by rolling its handle between your hands. You can also use a brush-spinning tool, an ingenious device that twirls the brush at high speed. Either way, the solvent will spray outwards; don't let it stain adjacent surfaces. After spinning the brush for the last time, straighten bristles and banish any remaining paint particles with a paintbrush comb.

Wrap: Unless you protect the cleaned bristles, they'll surely collect dust and debris before their next use. Wrap the bristles in a stiff paper keeper—the one that originally came with the brush—so they stay clean and straight (3). Store the brush flat or hang it up by the hole in its handle. Brushes for some types of latex paint require a dip in a water-rinsing solvent after a soap-and-water wash to rid the filaments of residue. Always check the "use and care" instructions on the back of the brush.

[leadpaint]

WHEN IT COMES TO WORKING WITH LEAD PAINT, TOM SILVA ADMITS he's done plenty of things wrong. "I used to burn it off woodwork and sand it until the air was filled with dust," says the *This Old House* general contractor, who's been in the business for 33 years. "The damage, if there is any, has already been done." Now, Silva's day of medical reckoning has arrived. He has volunteered for a study by the Harvard School of Public Health to calculate how much lead his bones have sopped up. (Lead is absorbed much like calcium, so bones become the record of past exposures.)

windows
and doors are the two biggest generators of lead dust. Maintain an intact coat of new paint over the old, and isolate sash from jambs with weatherstripping or plastic liners.

Using a sophisticated X-ray fluorescence analyzer, Harvard researchers have already found dangerously high levels of lead stored in the bones of dozens of other contractors and home owners; their levels registered high enough to put them at long-term risk of hypertension, anemia, kidney failure and memory loss. What will they find in Tom? Sitting in a chair at Boston's Channing Laboratory, he flips through a magazine as the X-ray analyzer zooms close to his shin. In thirty minutes, he will know.

Lead paint, long recognized as a health threat to young children in blighted urban housing, is now affecting a newly recognized set of victims: home renovators. "Some of the worst cases of lead poisoning I've seen involve whole families in which the parents buy a wonderful Victorian, roll up their sleeves, pull out the belt sander and grind away," says Dr. Howard Hu, an associate professor of occupational medicine who is running the Harvard study.

The full extent of the problem is not clear; no one keeps national records on poisonings caused by house paint. But in Massachusetts, a state known for its strict lead regulations, a report documented 380 cases of severe lead poisoning in construction workers from 1991 to 1995: 101 were housepainters and 172 were professional lead-paint abaters. Another 38 were home owners renovating their own houses. Richard Rabin, who coordinated the report, says this "grossly underestimates" the numbers of home owners likely to have high levels of lead in their blood. "If they're not

With its rhino-hide durability, ease of application and self-leveling smoothness, lead paint was the premier coating of its day. Those qualities came from powdered lead carbonate, which made up more than half the weight of some paints. Although lead was banned from use in house paints in 1978, a few industrial coatings, such as those used for striping roads, contain a small proportion of the toxic metal.

ACRYLI
EX
30 MINU
AINT
CAUTION!
CONTAINS LEAD
See other cautions
on back panel.
LOW VOC
IOR/EXTERIOR USE

[leadpaint]

tested, there are no statistics," he says.

Such poisonings are completely avoidable. Left undisturbed, lead-based paint is not a health hazard. You can rub your hand over it without danger; lead cannot be absorbed through skin. But sanding, scraping or burning off the paint creates clouds of lead-laced dust that can be inadvertently inhaled or swallowed. Rabin found that many people—even professionals—worked without respirators, ate their lunches without washing their hands and faces, and smoked cigarettes coated with lead dust. And the main dust culprits were power sanders: "With one of those, you can really do a job on yourself in a day or two," Rabin says.

Paints made before 1950 pose the greatest threat. Dr. Thomas Matte, an epidemiologist with the Centers for Disease Control and Prevention, says these paints often contain so much lead that the dust from a pulverized chip just one centimeter square can pollute a 10-by-20-foot room. "It's easy to see how a room could quickly be contaminated many times above the safe level," he says.

The ones most vulnerable to reckless renovating are not the guys with belt sanders but kids. A New York study showed that remodeling work was responsible for 10 percent of the elevated blood-lead levels in children statewide. Those less than 6 years old are most at risk; lead passes easily from their blood into their brains, causing long-term learning and hearing disabilities and reduced growth. Fortunately, our bodies naturally excrete lead, so blood-lead levels will gradually drop after exposure to the metal ends. Only in cases of serious poisoning is an expensive and protracted treatment called chelation used to quickly rid the bloodstream of lead. Unfortunately, there's no magic way to purge it from bones.

Given the dangers, getting a professional lead test is crucial. If lead is present, a home owner faces three basic choices: Live with it (and take some basic precautions), seal it off, or remove it. In many ways, the first approach is the best. "If your paint is in good condition, leave it alone." says Nick Farr, executive director of the National Center for Lead Safe Housing in Columbia, Maryland. "That's the surest way to protect yourself." Painted doors and windows need the most attention because they create minute amounts of lead-laced dust each time they rub against their jambs. Farr's organization has found, on average, about 11,000 micrograms of lead per square foot trapped in the troughs between the sash and the storms. "We've even found it as high as a million," he says. (A level below 800 micrograms is considered safe by HUD.) Farr recommends wiping interior sills with a wet cloth at least once a month; using an ordinary vacuum could spread a plume of dust. Old windows, often labeled as lead hazards and hauled off to landfills, can be retrofitted with plastic jamb liners or soft-pile weather stripping, both of which virtually eliminate the abrasion that generates paint dust.

The second option is encapsulation: burying lead in place. This involves coating woodwork with special lead-barrier paints or covering walls and ceilings with drywall or wainscoting. Merely applying a few coats of regular house paint is not sufficient. Although

test all *painted surfaces that will be affected by a remodeling. If there is a lead hazard, hire a certified contractor to remove it before remodeling starts.*

The $30,000 worth of lead abatement on this old house involved replacing 30 windows and scraping paint off much of the woodwork inside and out.

less expensive and less dusty than full-scale abatement, encapsulation does have its downside: The thick paints obliterate crisp architectural details, and the panels leave the poison for future renovators to uncover.

The third route—lead removal—is the most expensive, and if a remodeling is planned, the safest. This is a job for a state- or EPA-certified lead-abatement contractor—de-leading is not a do-it-yourself project. Even if you are protected with the right respirator, and disposable gloves and clothes, your family and neighbors are still at risk. A qualified lead-removal contractor has the equipment and, most important, the experience needed to do the work quickly and safely.

Complete removal is not always necessary: If a renovation is planned, only those surfaces that will be disturbed need to be stripped. Farr says remodeling contractors should take a cue from their lead-abatement brethren: "Create as little

« "If there's a lead problem, and there almost always is, I tell the home owner to get a licensed de-leader and have him deal with it." »

[leadpaint]

dust as possible, contain whatever is generated, and clean up well afterward."

Then, once the work is completed, a final series of independent wipe tests should confirm that everything is safe.

That's basically the approach Tom has taken in the last 10 years. "If there's a lead problem, and there almost always is, I tell the home owner to get a licensed de-leader and have him deal with it. I don't go near it," he says. If woodwork needs stripping, he prefers to have it removed and cleaned off-site; he avoids grinding, scraping or sanding painted surfaces as much as possible. On the *T.O.H.* renovation in Watertown, Massachusetts, he chose to rip off and replace the siding, rather than attempt the substantial job of sanding it smooth. "Why take the risk?"

Finally, the silent XRF aimed at Tom's leg has finished its scanning. With a click, the machine's shutter closes and a nearby computer screen flashes: 13 micrograms. "That's well within the normal range," says researcher Steve Oliveira. (A reading above 35 micrograms per gram of calcium would have been a problem.) Tom, relieved, takes a deep breath, then smiles. "I knew it would be," he says, as he heads off to another lead-safe day on the job.

A tarp taped to the foundation is ready to catch any lead-paint chips scraped from this house. Any chips must be disposed of as toxic waste.

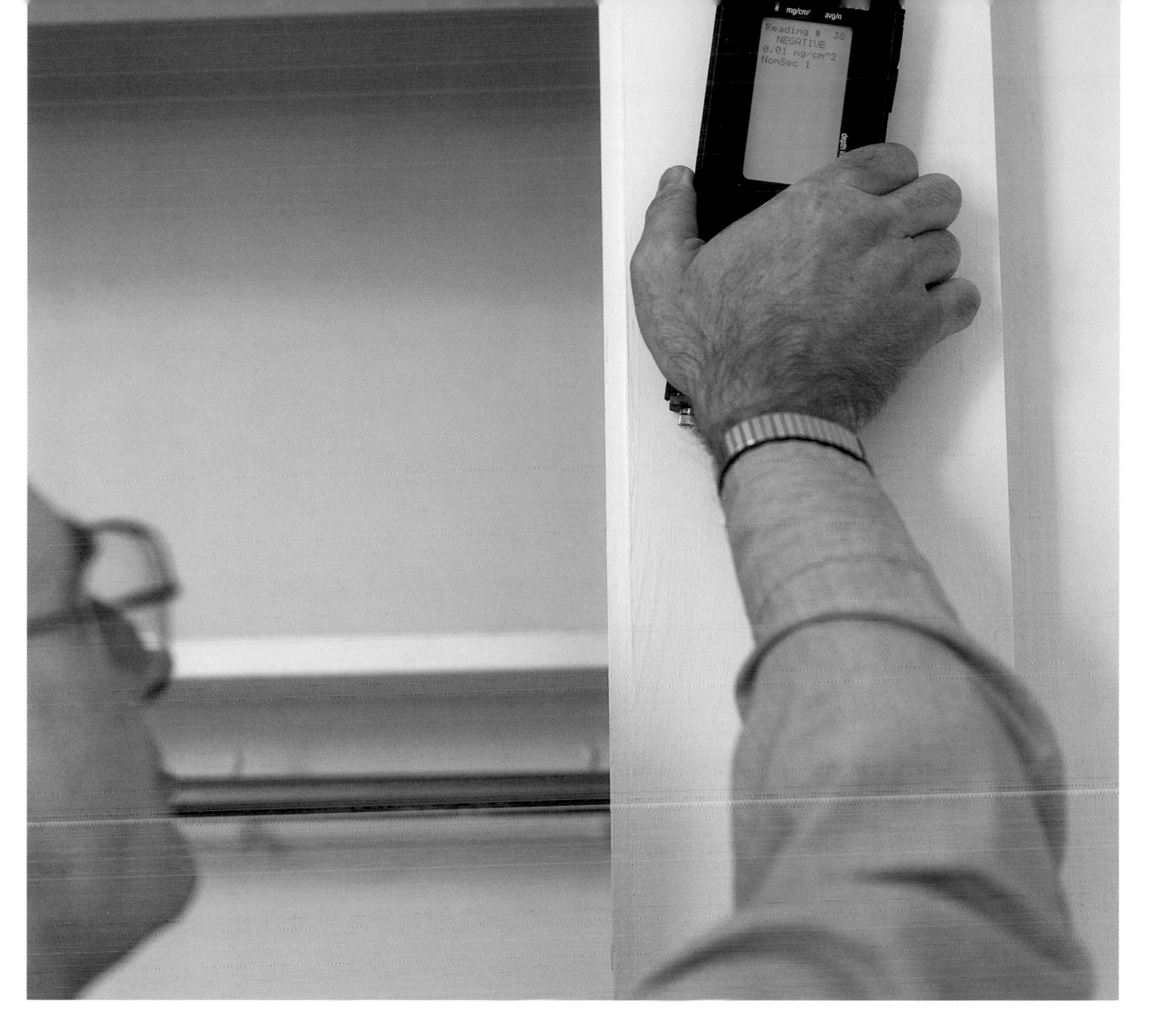

looking for lead

FINDING LEAD HAS GOTTEN FASTER, EASIER AND MORE ACCURATE, THANKS TO NEW TESTING TECHNOLOGY. AT ONE TIME, INSPECTORS RELIED ON A LABORATORY OR A CHEMICAL-SATURATED COTTON SWAB TO IDENTIFY LEAD PAINT. THOSE METHODS ARE STILL USED BUT HAVE THEIR DRAWBACKS. TRADITIONAL LAB TESTS, ALTHOUGH HIGHLY ACCURATE, CAN BE EXPENSIVE, AND REMOVING THE TEST SAMPLE LEAVES WOODWORK POCKED WITH LITTLE SQUARES. SWABS ARE CHEAPER AND FASTER—RUB ONE ON SUSPECT PAINT AND SEE IF THE TIP CHANGES COLOR—BUT CAN BE HARD TO INTERPRET AND ONLY DETECT THE LEAD THEY TOUCH, NOT HIDDEN LAYERS BELOW. THE NEWEST METHOD USES A CELL-PHONE-SIZED X-RAY FLUORESCENCE ANALYZER (XRF). HELD AGAINST A PAINTED SURFACE, THE DEVICE DISPLAYS HOW MUCH LEAD THE PAINT HAS AND HOW DEEPLY IT IS BURIED. THE COST FOR A WHOLE-HOUSE INSPECTION WITH AN XRF RUNS BETWEEN $200 AND $600 AND DOES NOT HARM WOODWORK.

[clear finishes]

IF YOU SPEND MONEY ON good wood, why slather the fact in paint? So goes the reasoning of those who prefer clear finishes on wood, whether on a strip oak floor, a tabletop or a beautiful band of crown molding. If you don't fancy paint, the alternatives include durable synthetic finishes such as urethane and natural products drawn from trees (tung oil) and bug sweat (shellac).

Those who abhor the thought of covering wood with urethanes liken it to coating the wood with plastic. "In residences," says architect Gary Brewer of New York's Robert A.M. Stern Architects, "we often specify a stain and then a shellac, then wax." But ask him what he specs for commercial wood floors with lots of foot traffic: "Oh, no question. You almost have to call out a urethane finish—nothing else will last." (There are esoteric molecular differences that distinguish a urethane from a polyurethane, but for all practical purposes the

Varnish. Natural or synthetic resins combined with oil (linseed, tung, safflower or soybean), petroleum-based solvents and metallic driers.

Penetrating oil. Tung oil or linseed oil in a petroleum-distillate solvent.

Oil-modified urethane. A combination of synthetic uralkyd resin, oils, petroleum-based thinners and metallic driers (cobalt, manganese, zirconium, zinc).

terms are interchangeable.) Here are the choices for clear wood finishing:

Oil-modified urethane leaves a thick, honey-toned surface that darkens with age. It is highly scratch-resistant once cured, withstands water and is relatively easy to apply but hard to touch up and recoat. The oil in it may be linseed (the most durable) or safflower or soybean (which don't yellow as much over time). The urethane-to-oil ratio determines the product's softness and flexibility: Less oil results in a harder finish.

A Master's Voice: Modern urethane coatings are simply the most durable protection you can put on a wood floor and still see the wood. Jeff Hosking, who is often seen refinishing worn floors on *This Old House*, offers the following flooring advice: 1. Before choosing a sheen, get a sample of gloss, semigloss or satin finishes applied to the same wood as your floor. 2. If you want a more natural wood look, use satin for the final coat. 3. Never damp-mop a wood floor. Clean with Windex instead, and wipe immediately.

Moisture-cured urethane. Urethane resins and solvents with dangerously flammable xylene solvent and toxic ketones.

Water-based urethane. Acrylic and/or urethane resins dispersed in water with solvents such as glycol ether.

Shellac. Non-toxic flakes from resin secreted by lac bugs, dissolved in denatured alcohol.

[clear finishes]

Varnish is one of the most beautiful of natural finishes, but it lacks the durability of a urethane. Varnishes based on long-oil (alkyd) formulations are more flexible and longer lasting than quick-drying, short-oil (phenolic) varnishes. Products with tung oil are easiest to apply and produce a smoother finish. Marine varnish contains ultraviolet inhibitors, which act as a sunscreeen to slow deterioration of the finish outdoors. The owners of mahogany boats apply 10 to 12 coats for a glossy finish, but painting contractor John Dee says three coats are sufficient for most outdoor woodwork on a house. Upkeep is a must: Depending on exposure, the finish should be lightly sanded every year, with one or two new coats applied.

The stench of decaying bug bodies is intense as factory workers in India use squares of muslin to retrieve kirilac, the lowest grade of shellac, from wash water.

Penetrating oil (sometimes called Danish oil) seeps into the wood rather than floating on the surface, making it a favorite for "touchable" wood such as furniture. Some products are based on tung oil (pressed from the nut of the Chinese tung tree) while others rely on linseed oil (a flax-seed extract); either may contain pigments. In order to add a protective layer to the wood, penetrating oils are typically covered with a buffable paste wax, making the surface time-consuming to maintain. Foods and common household products containing alcohol, vinegar or ammonia can discolor an oiled finish.

Moisture-cured urethane is the hardest, longest lasting and least yellowing (if aliphatic solvents are used) product on the market. It's the most stain-resistant finish, too, but is very toxic during application and should be applied only by professionals. A key ingredient (di-isocyanate methyl-benzene) cures the finish by pulling moisture from air.

Water-based urethane is the most popular floor finish. It dries in as little as an hour, making application convenient but tricky. Base resins can be acrylic (less durable) acrylic and polyurethane (very durable) or pure urethane (most durable) dispersed in water with solvents such as glycol ether, which may be extremely toxic.

Shellac is a resin that can be softened with heat and molded like clay, or dissolved in a solvent and spread whisper-thin. The least toxic clear finish, it gives a rich, warm appearance to wood. Though susceptible to water spotting and only moderately durable, a shellac finish is easy to touch up and dries quickly. Every bit of the substance comes from the sweat of tiny red bugs that live on tree branches in Asia; therein lies a tale.

Closely related to the insects that infest roses and other garden plants, *Laccifer lacca*

To preserve and protect exterior doors and trim from the elements without hiding the wood's beauty, take a tip from boaters: Use marine varnish. Also known as spar varnish, the coating's high oil content makes it more flexible than polyurethane, shellac or lacquer.

emerges live from its mother's body, crawls to a juicy stem, sinks in its mouth and through its skin secretes a thick substance—pure shellac. The goo hardens into a protective shell, and while males grow wings and fly out, females never move again. The bug is not particularly choosy about where it lives, but shellac is worth harvesting only where the climate allows the insects to thrive so that their crust forms a continuous mat on branches. And the economy must be so poor that villagers will laboriously scrape off the crust. Today, China and Thailand make some shellac, but only in India do thousands depend on it for their survival.

Villagers wade into vats of red goo that smell like manure to transform sticklac, the bug crust, into an industrial commodity. Sticklac is only about half pure shellac. Using machinery, workers grind the sticklac to the size of dried peas, sift out the bark and wash what's left in rotating drums or open concrete pits. Decaying bug bodies turn the wash water deep red, producing a dye that still colors Oriental carpets. Now called seedlac, the shellac resembles soggy Grape Nuts. Shellac leaves India as flakes or as seedlac.

The worlds biggest shellac firm, Wm. Zinsser & Co. of Somerset, New Jersey, sends much of the shellac it buys to its factory in Massachusets, and some ends up in cans of shellac. Most shelf space in hardware stores these days goes to urethanes. But along with its other traits, shellac contains no man-made (and potentially toxic) compounds. And the resource is endlessly renewable.

Although shellac flakes are still made by hand in many Indian factories, most of what's shipped to the West comes out of hydraulic presses and roller machines. But the process is still labor intensive. Women kneel at either side of the roller machine, pulling out the edges of the taffy-like shellac into a yard-wide ribbon.

A woman carries each section of pressed shellac across the room, letting it drift onto the floor to cool. Later, she will whack the ribbon with a willow branch, breaking it into pieces. The pieces are then packed into 110-lb. bags for shipment. When it leaves the factory, flake shellac is so fragile that it is hauled in refrigerated trucks: Too much heat or excess pressure will cause the thin, crisp flakes to meld into solid blocks.

WET PAINT
93/88 12/88 12/93

[interiorpainting]

"THE MOST important, most tedious—and therefore most neglected— WAY STATION ON THE JOURNEY TO PAINTING excellence is proper PREPARATION."

[preparingsurfaces]

A WALL'S LIFE ISN'T EASY. POKED, PUNCHED AND CRATERED BY EVERYTHING from thumbtacks to thrown toys, its pristine surface eventually succumbs to a steady rain of minor injustices. Whether the surface is plaster or drywall, a fresh coat of paint won't conceal problems; it will accentuate them. That's why professionals scrutinize a surface very carefully before they reach for a brush: A wall won't look good unless every imperfection that can be seen or felt has been patched. Modest damage to a wall—tight cracks, dents and holes less than the diameter of a quarter—can be repaired with layers of spackle. Major damage, including loose plaster, is another story.

DRYWALL: Gypsum rock quarried from the Midwest, Canada and Mexico is crushed, cooked, then mixed with water and additives. The slurry is compressed between paper skins.

While it may be tempting to rip down an old plaster-over-lath wall and replace it with drywall, often the plaster can be saved. Firm plaster that has popped off lath should be reattached with plaster washers and drywall screws. After removing areas that are crumbly, plasterer John Marshall patches holes with lime putty (a mixture of hydrated dolomitic lime, water, gauging plaster and a bonding agent) and a reinforcing layer of fiberglass mesh tape (see page 42). He trowels on the patch in two layers: a fill coat and a thin, final coat that can be blended so perfectly into the surrounding plaster that the patch, once painted, becomes invisible. A perfect patch, however, isn't necessarily perfectly smooth—like a chameleon, it must mimic its surroundings: "A plasterer's best tools," says Marshall, "are his arm and his eyes." Shallow patches can be primed with latex primer after a few hours; allow overnight drying if the patch is deep or if you're using alkyd primer.

Many people consider plaster the surface of choice, but these days most interior walls are clad in a material people love to hate: drywall. The ubiquitous product dates to the 1890s, when it was developed as a time-saving underlayment for coats of finish plaster. The cast panel of plaster reinforced with layers of felt paper ultimately evolved into the familiar half-inch gypsum/paper sandwich used today. Drywall is inexpensive and quick to apply, but furniture, fists, and even doorknobs that bounce off a plaster wall can poke though it with relative ease. If a hole is larger than a quarter, stuffing it with spackle won't suffice: Without reinforcement or solid backing, the dried glob just won't stay in place.

Tom Silva patches large holes in drywall with scraps of the same material reinforced

Clean water and fresh powder are essential plaster ingredients if you want the best results. Look for a date on the plaster bag, advises John Marshall; if plaster is more than 6 months old, don't use it.

TECHNIQUES

Preparing the plaster: A large area of damaged plaster, such as the example at left, calls for methodical preparation. Soft, crumbly plaster should be removed down to the lath and out as far as the firmly attached areas. Marshall chisels out the old plaster from between the lath and brushes away loose dust and plaster bits. Then he brushes a bonding agent over the lath and over any plaster that will be recoated, and bandages all but the smallest cracks with fiberglass mesh tape.

Making putty: Marshall mixes hydrated dolomitic lime with water, then slakes it (lets it rest undisturbed) for at least 20 minutes before adding a bonding agent and several handfuls of gauging plaster.

Reinforcing the patch: Marshall cuts a sheet of fiberglass mesh to cover the damaged area and presses it into a layer of wet plaster. The mesh reinforces the repair.

with window screening and joint compound. After cleaning loose drywall and any stray fringes of paper from the edges of the hole, he fits a similarly shaped scrap into the hole and screws it to the studs. Then he trowels joint compound over the area and embeds a clean, flat piece of fiberglass or aluminum window screen cut somewhat larger than the patch. When the joint compound is dry—usually the next day—he smooths on a second coat. After the hardened patch is sandpapered smooth, it's ready for paint. If he's in a rush, however, Tom stirs a bit of veneer plaster and water into the joint compound for the first layer. That makes it harden in 45 minutes instead of overnight.

Finishing it off: After the first coat sets, Marshall mixes another batch of putty and skims a thin, final coat over the entire area, using a sponge to erase surface blemishes.

***

REMOVING MOLD

MANY OF THE PARASITIC FUNGI COMMONLY KNOWN AS MOLD can be serious health hazards as well as being unsightly. As they feed on paper and other common materials in homes, molds produce compounds that may cause strong allergic reactions in 15 percent of the population. Some molds also produce poisonous compounds that can make anyone sick.

It's clear to many professionals, in fact, that there is a correlation between dampness or mold in houses and respiratory disease. But a homeowner's health isn't the only thing attacked by feral fungi—paint jobs suffer, too, particularly when someone trys to get rid of the problem by painting over it. That, says painter John Dee, will just make a bad situation worse. "It's tough to get at the source," he says, "once you've painted over it."

Mold and mildew are interchangeable names for thousands of species of filamentous fungi. Clusters of spores may be brown, black, green, blue, pink or white. Some look fuzzy, others slimy. The spores are the fruit of a mature mold whose weblike body, or mycelium, extends into porous surfaces much as tree roots extend into the earth. The microscopic spores (5 million would fit on the head of a pin) pose the biggest health concern because they are far more likely to be inhaled. Spores float easily and invisibly in air, collecting on walls, ceilings and other surfaces.

Molds grow at temperatures between 32 and 95 degrees Fahrenheit, but many species do best in the 70s and 80s. They require either water or a relative humidity above 60 percent in order to thrive. Most dead organic materials can supply food—even the oil in a fingerprint will do. Molds can digest the cellulose in paper but not the celluloses in wood. Thus, although they grow on and discolor paint and wood surfaces, they do not rot wood. As a byproduct of digestion, molds release volatile organic compounds which give molds their musty odors. If digestion stops, so does the smell. But the mold is only dormant, ready to resume feeding when conditions are suitable.

Painting over mildew doesn't mean it's gone—the sturdy spores are quite capable of growing right through a paint film later on. You'll have to get rid of mold before a surface is suitable for painting. For mold on a nonporous surface, such as old-fashioned plaster, the cleanup is relatively simple. First, set up a fan so it blows fresh air toward you. (If mold covers more than 10 square feet, tape off doorways in the room with plastic and set a fan in a window to blow air out while you are working.) You'll also need goggles, rubber gloves and a high-efficiency particulate air-purifying (HEPA) respirator equipped with a chlorine cartridge (see page 10). Using a bleach solution—one ounce ammonia-free detergent,

[preparingsurfaces]

one quart household bleach and three quarts water—wet each moldy spot for at least five seconds. Rinse the surface well and dump the wash water down the drain. Then go over every surface, including those you didn't wash, using a vacuum with a HEPA filter. (An ordinary vacuum will stir up lingering spores but won't remove them.)

For mold on a porous surface, such as drywall or carpeting, skip the bleach and remove the material itself if the infestation is serious. Keep the rest of the house clean by placing contaminated materials in double bags and lifting them out through windows (if possible) so as not to spread the problem.

To keep mold from coming back, cut off it's sustenance. In hot, humid climates, outside air is the primary source of moisture. In colder, drier climates, humidity often comes from within the house. Try simple cures, such as opening curtains on cold winter days so wooden muntins between window panes can dry. Leave the bathroom door open after a shower and take towels elsewhere to dry. Exhaust fans can also help, especially in bathrooms and the kitchen (make sure they vent to the outside, not into the attic). A portable dehumidifier may work, too. A $40 hygrometer, a device that measures relative humidity, can help you to adjust the dehumidifier so that it keeps the relative humidity below 60 percent.

To stave off outdoor mildew attacks, trim foundation shrubbery to improve air circulation. Remove tree branches that overhang the roof, too—shady spots encourage fungus growth. Some paints contain mildew inhibitors, but similar compounds can be added to regular paint as well.

most major *paint manufacturers offer mildew-resistant interior paints, often sold as "kitchen" or "bathroom" paint. These paints can stave off the onslaught of dreaded spores.*

another source of mold

UNTIL THE 1973 OIL EMBARGO AND THE SUBSEQUENT EMPHASIS ON ENERGY-EFFICIENT CONSTRUCTION, MANY HOUSES WERE SO DRAFTY THAT MOISTURE GENERATED INSIDE COULD ESCAPE. "WHEN THE BUILDING WAS NOTHING BUT PLASTER, YOU COULD BOIL SPAGHETTI ALL DAY LONG," SAYS RICHARD TRETHEWEY, THIS OLD HOUSE'S EXPERT ON INDOOR AIR QUALITY. "BUT THE MODERN HOME—THE HOME BUILT FROM 1975 ON—IS A TIGHT THERMOS BOTTLE. WHATEVER HUMIDITY WE CREATE CAN'T ESCAPE." TODAY, MANY HOMEOWNERS THINK THEY ARE PROTECTED BY THE DEHUMIDIFYING POWER OF AIR CONDITIONING AND CENTRAL HEATING. BUT THESE SYSTEMS CAN ACTUALLY INCREASE MOLD BECAUSE COLD AIR CANNOT HOLD AS MUCH MOISTURE AS WARM AIR. CONDENSATION CAN FORM WHERE WARM AIR TOUCHES A COLD SURFACE, SUCH AS ON THE UNDERSIDE OF AIR-CONDITIONED FLOORBOARDS.

FEW PEOPLE REALIZE THAT OVERSIZE AIR CONDITIONERS ARE PART OF THE PROBLEM. IF THE SYSTEM COOLS TOO FAST, IT DEHUMIDIFIES ONLY A SMALL PERCENTAGE OF THE HOUSE'S AIR, THEN SHUTS OFF. THIS LEAVES THE RELATIVE HUMIDITY HIGH AND OFTEN CAUSES CONDENSATION INSIDE DUCTS. IF THERE'S DUST IN THE SYSTEM TO SERVE AS FOOD FOR MOLD, THE FUNGI CAN GROW UNCHECKED IN THE VERY PLACES WHERE THEIR SPORES ARE MOST EASILY BLOWN THROUGH THE HOUSE.

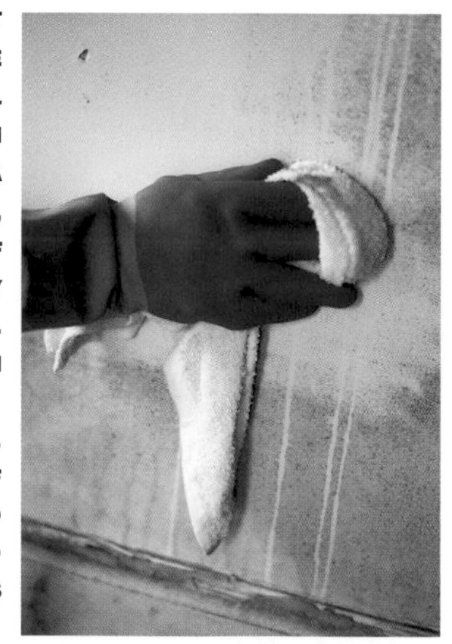

This professional cleanup crew first kills and then vacuums away mold, using a special vacuum that captures the tiniest of mold spores. Respirators and coveralls might seem excessive, but when there's a war on against widespread infestations, such gear is essential.

[maskingsurfaces]

ADHESIVE TAPE COMES IN A DIZZYING ARRAY OF WIDTHS, COLORS, materials and degrees of stickiness. Which roll to pick depends on the job: Some tapes must be waterproof, others have to resist changes in temperature. Permanent repairs require strong adhesives, temporary uses need less holding power. Paint masking tape, the ubiquitous tan roll, falls into the latter category.

Masking tape keeps paint in line, and away from where it ought not to be. The best stuff comes from painting stores; tape purchased elsewhere may look like true paint masking tape but might have several characteristics that render it useless for that job. Sometimes pseudo tape is too sticky; it leaves a tacky, paint-fouling residue behind or peels up a layer of paint when it departs. (Pulling tape off at an angle—and slowly—sometimes reduces this problem.) Cheap tape is often thicker, too, with edges that collect paint in a slurpy line that drips; better masking tape is thin.

Another reason for buying at a paint store is the selection: You'll find masking tape in rolls from ⅜-inch wide to 4 inches wide and more. But you'll also find other maskers, and one of them just might turn into your favorite. Some painters prefer paper-based masking tape, a wide, dark-brown roll that's only sticky

A Gaggle Of Tape: 1. Standard painter's masking tape comes in a variety of widths and lengths, all of it the same color: tan. Thickness and quality vary considerably, however. 2., 3. Some colored masking tapes offer nothing extra in the way of paint-masking; they're used primarily for color coding, labeling and decorative uses. 4. UV-resistant tape can be removed from glass even when left in direct sunlight for days at a time, a godsend for procrastinators.

1

2

on one edge. It goes on quickly and removes effortlessly. For bigger masking jobs there's masking film. By attaching thin plastic sheeting to its popular blue masking tape, one company made it possible to mask off large surfaces (such as wainscoting) prior to painting adjacent surfaces. It will also cover the inevitable gaps between wall and drop cloth—just stick the tape to the baseboard's top edge and unfurl the plastic sheet until it overlaps the dropcloth. The product dispenses from palm-size rolls that come in lengths of 25 or 30 yards, and the film is available in three different widths up to 35 inches. Or perhaps you prefer a more traditional alternative: taping up sheets of yesterday's newspaper or scraping little blobs of paint off the floor.

If spraying is in your painting plan, you may need more masking than a roll of tape can muster: You may have to mask off an entire section of a room. One manufacturer provides a set of lightweight telescoping poles for just this purpose. In just a few minutes, the four poles and a little plastic sheeting can create the next best thing to a true hermetically sealed work area, so sawdust and plaster dust (and paint spray) won't have a chance to infiltrate the rest of the house. You could also, of course, staple plastic sheets to a homemade frame of 2x4s; in either case, however, be sure to leave an opening for ventilation.

TECHNIQUES

Mask it: Tape-and-plastic is the best way to protect large surfaces from paint splatter. First, press the tape against a surface, such as the chair rail shown here.

Paint away: Smooth down the tape with a finger to run out any air bubbles, then coax out the plastic and let it cascade over the wall. Grab a brush and get to work.

3

4

[painting walls]

JOHN DEE, PAINTER, IS passionate about his craft yet disciplined in his painting technique. Determined to get the best paint job he can in any room, he's methodical about every task from wall prep to cleanup. Such efforts pay off: He can make a room look as if it had been lifted from a house, dipped in paint and returned. In his years as a professional, Dee has developed a reputation that keeps his schedule full and his arm in constant motion.

working from *a ladder is impractical for rolling paint. Instead, Dee always screws an extension pole into his roller frame when painting ceilings and walls. "I get a better view that way too."*

Each project Dee tackles presents a unique set of problems, but his emphasis on wall preparation ensures consistant solutions whether he's painting a closet or every wall in every room of a 10,000 square-foot house.

Dee's first step on any paint job is to make some space to work. He either moves all the furniture into another room, or huddles it in the middle of the room and covers it with plastic sheeting. "I need a three-foot perimeter of working space all the way around," he explains. Once the room is safe, Dee unscrews or pries off any hardware, saving it if possible for later reinstallation.

On this project, as on many he has faced, wallpaper had to be stripped from the old plaster walls before he could even see the walls. Stripped walls need a day to dry, and then there's an hour's worth of preparation to protect the floor with heavy-duty rosin paper, a chore he regards as cheap insurance: "Removing dried paint from a wood floor is a nuisance and completely avoidable." After all the preparation, Dee is ready to roll.

ROLLER COVER: This fuzzy cylinder carries paint to the wall. The most versatile cover is 9 inches long and has a 3/8-inch-thick polyester-fiber nap for painting smooth surfaces with flat latex. A 3/4-or 1-inch nap is best for painting textured ceilings.

BRUSH: For cutting in on walls, Dee uses a 2 1/2- or 3-inch wide nylon-poly brush with a square edge.

ROLLER SPINNER: Dee whirls paint and water off roller covers as part of his cleaning routine. Spinners can also handle brushes.

ROLLER TRAY: Metal trays are best—plastic trays are too hard to clean. When working with different colors but only one metal tray, fit the tray with a disposable plastic liner.

MASKING TAPE: Durable, UV-resistant tape protects baseboard and secures protective paper to wood floors. It's expensive, but will stick for weeks and won't lift a floor finish when removed.

5-IN-1 TOOL: Serves as a scraper, paint-lid opener, roller cleaner, crack-opener, and crude nail setter. This one even has a teardrop hole in the blade for pulling nails.

ROLLER FRAME: Dee uses heavy-gauge frames such as this one; some models have clips that hold covers tightly yet allow easy removal. A 9-inch frame is his standard. Smaller frames help where space is tight; 18-inch frames are useful for unusually large walls and ceilings.

[paintingwalls]

once all prep *is complete, Dee generally follows this painting agenda: ceilings first, then all trim and finally the walls.*

TECHNIQUES

Soaking Wallpaper: Before he could paint this project, Dee had to remove wallpaper by misting the walls with a mild stripper solution. First, he pried up a seam and pulled on the paper "to see what I'm in for." To ready for spraying, Dee protects floors by tripling the edge of a canvas drop cloth directly against the baseboards, spreading the rest several feet into the room. He mists walls from top to bottom, using a flap of cardboard to protect the ceiling from spray. His mantra: "Get the walls wet, wet them again and keep them wet." Dee sprays each wall three times, always stopping a few inches short of the baseboard to reduce runoff. The stripper is mild enough for Dee to work without a wearing a respirator or gloves—as long as he can ventilate the room by opening a window.

Stripping Wallpaper: Paper that releases easily when Dee pries on a seam will probably come off in full sheets coaxed by gentle, two-handed tugs; otherwise, it will have to be scraped off. Dee guides his scraper like a snowplow. "Choose one side of the scraper and stick with it for the life of the blade," he says, and it will glide over walls. "Flipping it back and forth develops hooks in the blade and makes it more prone to gouging." Heavy-duty papers, foils and mylars tend to hug the wall and some vinyls may not budge from their paper backs. In that case, Dee rolls a small, inexpensive scoring tool over the paper before spraying it; the tool perforates the surface just enough to allow stripper to penetrate. Some people score vinyl paper by drawing a hand saw over the surface, but Dee discourages this approach: "It kills the saw."

Prepping Walls: When the wallpaper is gone, Dee sprays more stripper on the walls and uses a damp sponge to lift off any remaining adhesive. "If I don't get the glue," he says, "new paint will reactivate it and the paint's bond can suffer." Dee's prep regimen is straightforward and simple if the walls are in good shape. Cracks and minor damage are filled with a mixture of patching plaster and Plaster of Paris (deep cracks should be coated first with a bonding agent). Dee sands patched areas by hand or with a pole-sander, using 120-to-150 grit paper, and caulks joints between casings and the walls. If the patching is extensive (or before a dramatic color change, or when painting over a glossy surface), Dee primes the walls with one coat of an acrylic primer-sealer. If the wallpaper concealed a textured surface, such as the horsehair plaster walls of this project, Dee skim-coats them twice with joint compound and then sands, primes again and caulks. The extra work would aggravate anxious painters, but Dee is patient: "If I don't skim, I won't get a smooth surface to roll paint over."

Masking Baseboards: Dee paints all the woodwork in a room before he rolls the walls—he finds cutting walls into painted trim easier than the reverse. But this approach works only if there's time for the trim to dry overnight before the walls are painted. To protect painted baseboards (and the top of the room's thermostat) from being speckled or smeared by wall paint, Dee masks them with UV-resistant tape. Starting at a corner of the baseboard, he pulls out about a foot at a time and lays it against the top of the wood, sealing the tape as he goes with a swipe of his fingernail. "A lot of people don't bother to mask off," Dee says, "because it takes too much time and the tape is expensive." But it's a step Dee would never skip. To protect wood floors, Dee uses the same masking tape to secure a border of red rosin paper (a floor underlayment) around the room.

[paintingwalls]

when using *the same paint within two or three days, Dee tightly wraps paint-soaked roller covers in plastic. "They can survive this way for days, and it beats washing them out each time."*

Cutting In: "Cutting in is the thing do-it-yourselfers fear most," says Dee, especially when using contrasting paint colors on walls and trim. Masking tape and edging tools can help, and Dee does not discourage their use. "You can get a good clean line that way, but if you've worked with a brush for 25 years, as I have, you'd be a klutz with an edger." Before he picks up a paintbrush, Dee lightly sands primed surfaces with 150-grit paper to smooths the surface. Ready to paint, Dee dips his brush about an inch into the can, pats one brush face and scrapes excess paint off the other, making the brush drip-free. He edges gradually around the door casing and then along the ceiling line using smooth, steady strokes, not short choppy ones: "Accuracy is the bottom line when cutting in, not speed," he says. Dee stretches the paint back and forth, working first toward and then away from the wet edge. To elimininate brush marks, Dee always ends a stroke on the wet edge but never starts one there. "If you start a brush stroke on a dry surface and terminate it at the wet edge, it is less likely to show when it dries," he explains.

Tackling the Details: Dee cuts in with the edge of his brush, not the side, in order to get a crisp line. After cutting in along casings, he cuts in around at the room's corners and around details such as electrical boxes and radiators. Whenever paint is brushed on a surface, a line forms on the edge of the stroke. To prevent lines from drying in place and creating ridges, Dee returns with a slightly dry brush to the small sections he has cut in and picks up the excess paint. This extra step feathers out the paint and will help it blend in once the walls are rolled. To paint the wall behind radiators, Dee often uses a 6 inch "hot dog," a slender roller cover mounted on a long-handled roller frame. The cover's small diameter enables it to reach places inaccessible to standard-diameter covers.

Rolling the "W": Dee starts rolling near the top of a wall and works his way down to eliminate drips. He picks up paint from a tray on the floor, lifts his roller and paints a "W" to load paint on the wall. On his next pass, he presses lightly on the roller to stretch out the "W" and distribute the paint over about 15 square feet. Near door casings, Dee rolls in as tightly as he can, overlapping the brushed areas, and then rolls out into the open field of the dry wall, distributing the paint into a rectangle. He makes a final pass with a light stroke ending in the middle of the wall, where he pulls the roller away. "The paint should defy gravity," says Dee: If it drips down the wall after application, the coat was too thick. But too little paint will produce a sandlike texture that dries to an uneven sheen. As he paints, Dee continually checks the walls for holidays—areas imperfectly covered—and takes care of them before moving on: "Going back over an area that has begun to set up causes lap marks." The raking light from a window, or from Dee's 500-watt halogen worklight, makes holidays easier to locate and cover.

Rolling Walls: As he works from top to bottom, Dee moves across the wall, constantly on the lookout for holidays and drips. By mounting his roller on an extension pole Dee minimizes backbreaking hours of bowing down and stretching up to paint, and gets a better perspective on how the work is going. A 9-inch roller is standard issue for Dee; bigger rollers are too wide to follow the contours of the bulging or rippled surfaces common in older houses. Polyester fiber is the most commonly used roller cover material, but quality and strength vary: Cheap rollers shed easily, and their cardboard cores often don't last through an entire job. A good roller has a phenolic core, sheds little, and holds up to repeated washing. Mohair covers have very tight naps, useful for thinner coats and glossier oils and varnishes.

Cleaning Up: Dee cleans a roller by squeezing off paint with a "5-in-1" tool (above). Then he rinses the roller in dishwashing soap and water, using the spinner (right) to whirl off residue into a bucket so it doesn't fly everywhere.

The lively finished den (right) is the reward for Dee's meticulous work. In a well-painted room, the lines are crisp and well-defined, surfaces are smooth and joints are tight. Unpainted surfaces are free of paint specks and there's no trace of the painter's labors.

[sandpaper]

IN NATURE, GARNET IS A gorgeous deep red, its crystals clumped against a sparkling background of black hornblende streaked with white feldspar. No wonder the best specimens are set in gold, made into jewelry and prized as January's birthstone. More ordinary garnet crystals, though, are destined for duty in the most utilitarian of tools: sandpaper. A century after the first synthetic abrasives were invented, garnet sandpaper still figures prominently in many hardware store displays. We reach for it because it's what our fathers used, and because it works. But garnet isn't always the best product for sanding.

sanding blocks *are good for leveling a surface, but sandpaper used by itself is more effective at scuffing paint. Sanding sponges work beautifully for hand sanding curved surfaces.*

Garnet wears down faster than synthetic abrasives such as aluminum oxide and silicon carbide, so it's never used in the more highly engineered sandpapers sought out by professionals, including painters. These sandpapers don't work better just because they have different abrasives: The type of backing, the kind of adhesive that holds the abrasive to it and the frequent presence of special coatings are at least as important.

For example, there's a light-green paper that minimizes clogging even on water-based finishes and polyurethanes. Its secret is not its abrasive (aluminum oxide, invented in 1897) but a soaplike coating that will slough off, carrying sanding debris with it. Norm Abram raves about a different aluminum oxide product for his random-orbit sander. He knows it as "micron paper," after the dimension used to measure grit size. First developed for the computer industry, micron papers have a waterproof polyester film base, used because the superfine particles needed to polish parts would sink into paper or cloth. Grit size is closely controlled, so virtually all grains are the same size, compared with up to 50 percent "filler" particles in standard sandpaper. The better backing and more uniform sizing give Norm the finish he wants faster.

Virtually all abrasives are crystals that break down during use, exposing sharp, fresh surfaces with every stroke. Abrasives are rated on two qualities—toughness (how hard it is to get the crystals to break) and hardness (how resistant they are to wearing

Garnet is sorted for size by shaking the crystals through a series of progressively finer screens, in a decidedly low-tech process.

Garnet from the Adirondack Mountains, like these circular clumps, works well in sandpaper because numerous fissure planes make it crumble easily. Jewel-quality garnet is a deep burgundy and contains fewer fissure lines.

[sandpaper]

down). Abrasives are only part of the sandpaper story, however. All those cutting and clawing crystals have to be stuck to something or they'll be little more than stock for sandcastles.

What they're stuck to is the backing, and the stiffer it is, the faster sandpaper will cut. That's why you should select a product that's only flexible enough to conform to the shape being sanded. To increase the effective stiffness of thin sandpaper, wrap it over a sanding block—a short scrap of smooth wood that fits comfortably in your hand—or a sanding pad.

The third basic element of sandpaper is the adhesive: that's what joins abrasive to backing. Sandpaper has two layers of adhesive, one to anchor the abrasive grains and a second to lock them in place. The choices are two coats of hide glue, two coats of resin or a coat of resin over hide glue. Hide glue generally sets faster and is more flexible, but resin is better at resisting moisture and heat. Paper with hide glue works well for sanding complex shapes, but moisture—even high humidity—can make it virtually useless. For power sanding and sanding with a lubricant, go for resin-based paper. Resin over hide glue produces sandpaper that starts out and stays sharpest the longest. Though many other characteristics are typically identified on the back of a sheet of sandpaper, the type of adhesive type is rarely specified. One test is to exhale close to the surface and then sniff: If it stinks, the sandpaper contains hide glue.

« Virtually all abrasives are crystals that break down during use, exposing fresh, sharp surfaces. »

Silicon carbide, the second most common abrasive, is harder than aluminum oxide and produces a smoother surface on wood. It's the best choice for sanding between tough finish coats. Lubricate fine grits with water or oil to keep the sharp slivers from clogging up before they wear down. It can also be used on nonferrous metals.

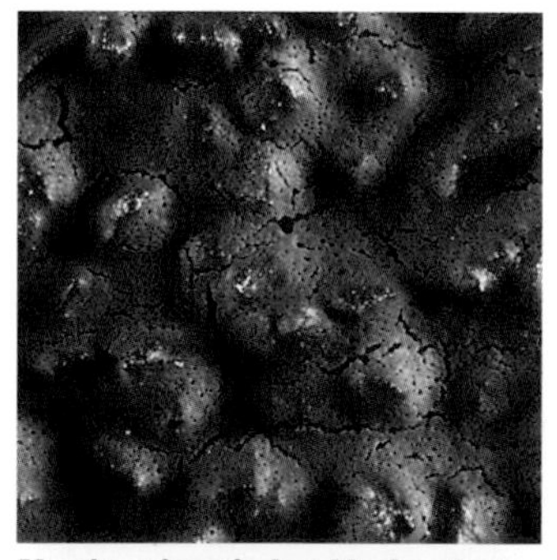

Alumina zirconia has blocky, sharp crystals that remove a lot of material fast. It's a good abrasive for shaping and grinding wood and metal, but not for polishing. Made from oxides of aluminum and zirconium, it's often sold in wide "planer" belts that sand boards to a desired thickness.

Diamond is the hardest abrasive, and it's excellent for shaping and smoothing metal, glass and other hard materials. Made with synthetic diamonds to reduce cost, it still runs about $2 per square inch. The dot pattern shown here minimizes clogging by allowing plenty of room for sanding debris.

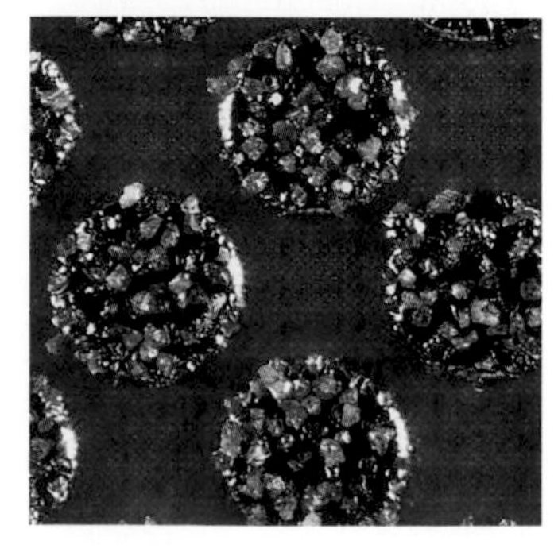

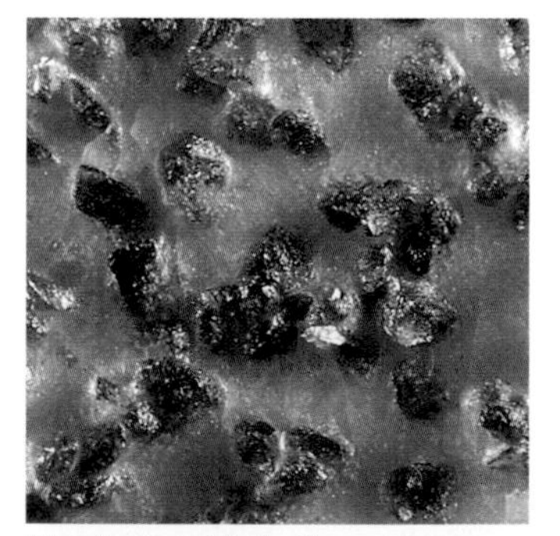

Aluminum oxide is the most common general-purpose abrasive for wood and metal. First made in about 1897 from bauxite, the formula can be varied to produce crystals with very different characteristics. Here they are wedge-shaped (and embedded in a thick resin) to stand up well against the rigors of floor sanding.

BREAKING A CODE. 1. PRODUCT NUMBER: THIS ENABLES A USER TO REORDER THE EXACT SANDPAPER OR LEARN MORE ABOUT ITS CHARACTERISTICS FROM THE MANUFACTURER. 2. ABRASIVE: NATURAL ABRASIVES ARE USUALLY LISTED, BUT SYNTHETICS ARE OFTEN IDENTIFIED BY TRADEMARKED NAMES. 3. BACKING: MOST HAND SANDING SHEETS ARE BACKED WITH PAPER. "A" WEIGHT, THE LIGHTEST, IS FOR HAND SANDING WITH FINE GRITS. "C" AND "D" WEIGHTS ARE FOR HAND AND LIGHT POWER SANDING OF WOOD AND DRYWALL. OTHER BACKING OPTIONS INCLUDE CLOTH (MOST COMMON FOR HOME USE IS "J" WEIGHT, ALSO CALLED JEANS CLOTH), FIBER AND POLYESTER FILM. 4. OPEN COAT: SOMETIMES ABBREVIATED OC, THIS MEANS ABRASIVE PARTICLES COVER 40 TO 70 PERCENT OF THE SURFACE (CLOSED- COAT PAPERS ARE COMPLETELY COVERED). OPEN-COAT PAPERS CLOG LESS QUICKLY BUT LEAVE A ROUGHER SURFACE. 5. SAFETY WARNING: YES, A DISC CAN FLY OFF A SANDER OR A SANDING BELT CAN BREAK. 6. GRIT SIZE: 100 GRIT MEANS PARTICLES PASSED THROUGH A SCREEN WITH 100 OPENINGS PER INCH (10,000 PER SQUARE INCH), BUT NOT THROUGH A FINER SCREEN. A "P" BEFORE THE NUMBER SIGNALS A MORE RESTRICTIVE EUROPEAN STANDARD. 7. LOT NUMBER: THIS IDENTIFICATION ENABLES THE MANUFACTURER TO TRACE ANY SHEET TO THE TIME AND CONDITIONS UNDER WHICH IT WAS MANUFACTURED, USEFUL IF PROBLEMS DEVELOP.

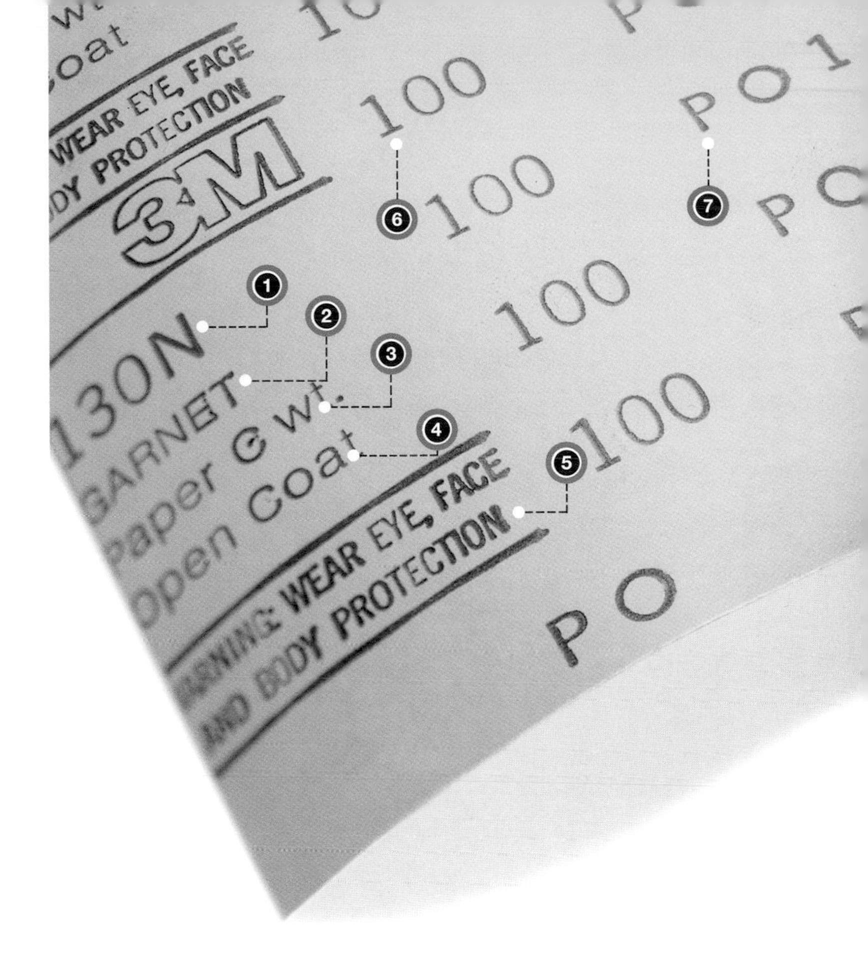

how to read sandpaper

Emery is good for polishing metal, but it's unsuitable for use on wood because the edges of the crystals tend to dull rather than chip. It's a combination of corundum (a natural aluminum oxide) and iron oxide, and is usually used with an oil lubricant to flush debris away.

Crocus is a natural or synthetic iron oxide, mixed with a small amount of silicon dioxide. Like emery, crocus is used to clean and polish metal. But crocus is considerably softer than emery, so it is used where only very slight stock removal is desired. The same abrasive is the basis of rouge, used to polish metal.

Garnet is the softest common abrasive. Crystals fracture under light pressure, so garnet works well for hand sanding of wood. It's probably the best option for difficult power sanding jobs where other papers might burn the wood, such as sanding the end grain of hardwood. Garnet is unsuitable for sanding metal.

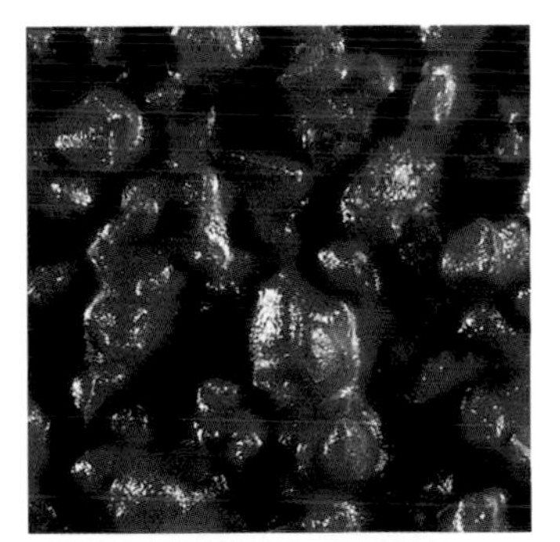

Ceramic aluminum oxide is a relatively new kind of aluminum oxide that's much tougher than standard and has a more uniform crystalline structure. Use it to power-sand metal, wood and many other materials (professional floor sanders use it a lot). It is often mixed with regular aluminum oxide for use on sanding belts.

[paintingtrim]

FEET PLANTED, A BURLY arm extended, painter John Dee presses his brush against the door and begins to bow. The action suggests obeisance at a Shinto shrine, but when asked, Dee picks a less reverent analogy: "I look like a figurine on a cuckoo clock." Sublime or ridiculous, he bends in service to his craft. "If you make the movement with the large muscles of the waist, instead of the arm, you get a truer vertical stroke," Dee says. Sure enough, the ocher swath he applies to the stile is as sharp and straight as the centerline of a new highway.

"there is no *pride in preparing wood for paint," says John Dee. "You just do whatever has to be done for the quality level you're shooting for—no more, no less."*

Among the construction arts, painting is the least likely to receive this kind of in-depth analysis. Plumbers, electricians and general contractors all hold licenses, so their skills command respect, Dee points out. Meanwhile, he observes with gentle forbearance, "most people think they can paint." But painting doesn't differ from finish carpentry: Only specific, exacting, time-tested techniques will yield a fine product. Dee says that's particularly true of repainting interior trim: woodwork such as doors, windows and balusters are the most difficult challenges he faces. A full-time painter for nearly three decades, Dee has honed his brushwork to achieve what he half-jokingly terms the obsessive-compulsive finish. "If you take a perfect, smooth, shop-sprayed lacquer job as your ideal—and aim for that—you won't achieve it," he concedes. "But if you shoot for perfect, you'll hit excellent. That's a good place to be." So why not take a door off its hinges and spray paint it with something like an HVLP sprayer? Sometimes, he says, he'll do that (see page 68). "But it's almost too slick, especially in older houses. I like the hand-done look of brushed-out woodwork."

The most important, most tedious—and therefore most neglected—way station on the journey to painting excellence is proper preparation. First, Dee determines how well the existing layers of paint stick to one another and to the underlying wood. He probes peeling paint with a putty knife. If he finds a weak link between the second and third coats of a seven-layer finish, for example, he'll concentrate on strip-mining down to coat two.

Even an apparently pristine paint surface can hide weak adhesion below. Dee tests unobtrusive areas by mashing down a 4-inch-square section of duct tape, then jerking it away (see page 67). At one particular job, a 1903 Georgian-style house in Concord, Massachusetts, the tape peeled up silver-dollar-sized chips of old paint. "See?" he says. "The

Painting balusters is ideally a job for two people, one on each side, to arrest any drips or lap marks. When John Dee works solo, he paints no more than six balusters on one side before painting the other side.

Dusting with a tack cloth—the last step before wetting the brush—picks up the sanding residues and bits of dirt that even vacuum cleaners miss. Dee spends a mere 50 cents or so on each cloth, and he says one cloth can clean all the woodwork in a good-sized living room before losing its stick. That's cheap insurance for a top-notch finish.

blue coat isn't adhering to the buff coat underneath." Because that house, like many built before lead paint was banned in 1978, undoubtedly contained strata of toxic finish, Dee donned a respirator and full-body coveralls. He sealed the work area with plastic sheeting and duct tape before he started to scrape.

On flat areas, he uses a razor blade in a wallpaper scraper and pushes it until he can no longer persuade paint to come up. With a pull scraper, he then digs out the grooves where the door panels meet the stiles and rails. After shaving away most of the offending paint layers, Dee begins to sand. On the fun meter, sanding paint ranks somewhere between a tax audit and tattoo removal, so it's a fair bet that most weekend painters skip this step—a huge mistake, says Dee. Sanding, he explains, ensures that paint will adhere and eliminates the drips, runs and brush marks (called rope) left by less skilled predecessors. "I typically use a random-orbit sander on the flats and then hand-sand the moldings," he says. Though Dee recommends sanding all wood surfaces before painting, sanding intricately detailed pieces (such as the balusters on page 61) could actually do more damage than good by removing some of the detail or rounding over crisp edges. That's when he'll wipe de-glosser

The bits of dried paint and grunge that collect in opened paint cans will inevitably ruin a finish. When Dee uses paint from previous jobs, he always filters it (left) through a paper funnel (with mesh at the bottom) into a pristine can.

TECHNIQUES

First, the panels: Dee painted this door as he would any paneled woodwork. He starts on the moldings surrounding the panels, then paints the panels themselves (1). While applying paint, he pulls the finish away from the edges and corners where it might collect in drip-prone gobs.

Then stiles and rails: Dee paints across the joints between stiles and rails (2), rather than ending his strokes abruptly, in order to avoid leaving behind an ugly moraine of paint. Once the paint is evenly distributed in an area, he uses just the tip of his brush to smooth it gently in the direction of the wood grain.

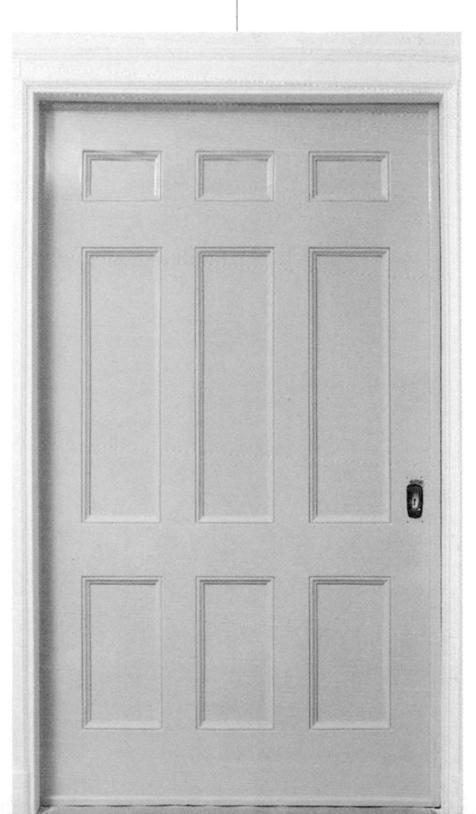

[paintingtrim]

THE BASIC STEPS THAT APPLY TO PAINTING DOORS ALSO HOLD TRUE FOR DOUBLE-HUNG WINDOWS, AND THEN SOME. "ALWAYS PAINT THE UPPER SASH FIRST," DEE SAYS. "THAT WAY, YOU CAN MOVE THE LOWER SASH AND NOT MESS UP THE PAINT." ALSO, HE DELIBERATELY LEAVES A THIN LINE OF PAINT ON THE GLASS AS HE WORKS, BUT HE DOESN'T WAIT FOR THE PAINT TO DRY BEFORE SCRAPING IT: SCRAPING DRIED PAINT LEAVES RAGGED, PEEL-PRONE EDGES. INSTEAD, HE PLACES A STRAIGHT-EDGED RAZOR BLADE FLAT AGAINST THE GLASS AND GENTLY PLOWS THE WET PAINT INTO THE GAP BETWEEN WOOD AND GLASS. IN ONE STEP, HE GETS A CLEAN EDGE AND A GOOD SEAL WITH THE GLASS. "IT'S THE BEST WAY TO DO IT," HE SAYS.

painting a window

over the surfaces instead. De-glosser is a potent liquid solvent that cleans and softens a layer of paint so the new coat can bond to it. It can be purchased in pint cans.

Dee is a felicitous combination of craftsman and hard worker, however, so he never hesitates to use muscle power if that's what will get the best results. "On some restoration jobs," he says with a hint of pride, "I spend as much as 75 percent of my time on preparation." Such meticulous care shows in the finished surface.

Most doors succumb to a thorough random-orbit sanding. In 45 minutes of steady, sweaty exertion, he smooths the door with 100-grit sandpaper followed by an aggressive round of 150-grit stroking: tough love. After brushing aside furrows of sanding dust, Dee fills any gouges or small holes in the wood with vinyl spackling. Because the stuff shrinks as it dries, he saves time by mounding it slightly above the surface, then sanding it flush when it hardens. (If he spread it flush using a putty knife, he'd have to go back and refill the sunken areas after the first layer dried.)

Finally, after all the sanding is complete, Dee thoroughly vacuums the door's surface, then wipes it down with a sticky, dust-collecting handkerchief known as a tack cloth.

Can we paint now?

Not quite. Dee gives unopened cans of paint and primer a vigorous shake before stirring them. With previously opened cans, he

Painting indoors or out, understand the surface you're dealing with. The white lead trim on this house, for example, would be hazardous to scrape or sand.

[paintingtrim]

fishes out any paint skin with his stir stick, then filters out dirt, bugs and dried bits of paint with a 17-cent disposable paint strainer. Panty hose also work, though they won't hold a funnel shape as nicely.

For his first coat, Dee brushes on an enamel underbody primer, the product he likes most to use over old paint. (On bare wood, he uses a primer-sealer instead.) "It's always a good idea to prime, especially if you've done all that sanding," says Dee. To top-coat woodwork, he prefers alkyd (oil-based) paint to water-based latex: "I find that it levels better. It dries more slowly and keeps a wet edge longer." He applies the alkyd with a good quality nylon-polyester brush 2½ inches wide with a flat cut as opposed to an angled one. (For more on brushes, see page 24.) Synthetic filaments hold less paint than natural bristles do but, he says, "With bristles, I'm forever picking broken ends out of the paint."

Dee starts by painting the door panels, working each one from the edge to the center. "I'm constantly pulling the paint out of the sides, where it wants to collect," he says. Unevenly distributed paint is a major cause of rope, as are overworked latex and underworked oil. Once he fills a panel with horizontal and diagonal strokes, he "tips off" with a relatively paint-free brush. Starting at the top of a panel, he pulls the brush down and back up once, gently leveling the surface.

As Dee finishes each panel, he reaches for the loop of his painter's pants, where he keeps a cotton rag slightly dampened with thinner, and wipes the surrounding stiles and rails clean. He follows his fundamental painting rule: If he cannot keep a wet edge, he makes sure that wet and dry edges meet at a sharp corner. Otherwise, slopped-over paint dries and forms unsightly raised areas.

When all the panels are done, he paints the stiles and rails. He begins at the door's top, spreading the paint in all directions, then tips off only in the direction of the wood grain. Adhering to the maintain-the-wet-edge rule, he paints and tips off all the way to the bottom, covering both stiles and rails as he goes. Dee takes care not to lap paint back onto the panels or the molded edges, however. "If you weren't that steady, you could let the panels dry first. Then if anything slopped on the panels, you could wipe it off."

The door done and glistening, Dee pauses to admire his work. The care he lavishes is evident. Even from 10 feet away, the painted surfaces impress: smooth, clean, elegant. But Dee's quest for perfection can backfire, as it did when he painted the front door for a *This Old House* project in Salem, Massachusetts. "It was my first time working with the show, and I wanted to make a good impression." When he finished, visitors could almost see their reflections in the door's glassy black surface. Later, however, a member of Salem's historical commission reprimanded home owner Deborah Guinee for having a metal door in an area where only wood was allowed. Guinee had to set the misguided commissioner straight by proving that the door was wood. "Making the door as smooth as metal wasn't my aim," says Dee with a grin. "I just wanted to show what we could do with paint."

TECHNIQUES

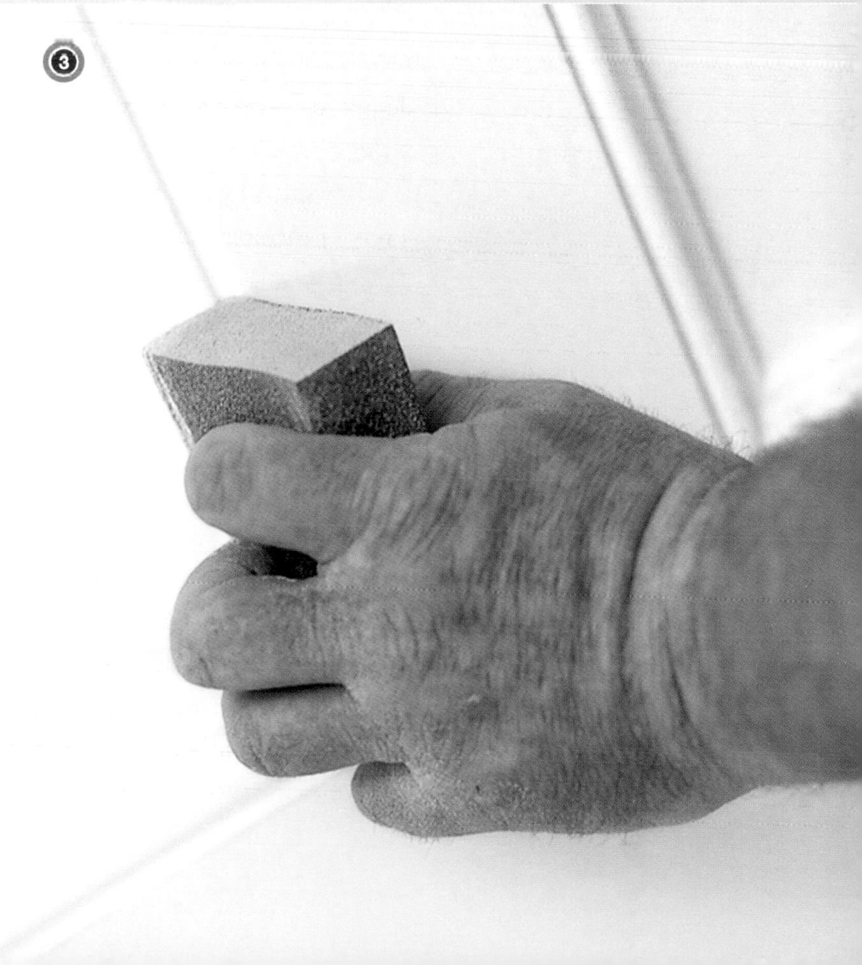

Investigate: There's more to removing paint than clawing away at it with sharp, stiff blades. Before scraping, Dee tries to determine how well paint is adhering to a surface, and he doesn't need fancy equipment to find out: He just squashes down a piece of duct tape and pulls it back (1) to see what has stuck to the bottom. This test shows Dee how many layers he has to scrape off.

Scrape: Dee push-scrapes the flat areas of a door with a wall-paper remover and pull-scrapes along the panel's edges, where paint buildup is particularly acute. His pull scraper (2) for detail work has a long-lived tungsten carbide blade with three cutting edges. A fresh edge can be rotated into place whenever one dulls. (For more on scraping paint, see page 98.)

Sand: A scraped surface must (alas) also be sanded. Dee's favorite sanding tools include a flexible foam sanding sponge (3) for the curves on molding, and open-coat silicon carbide sand-papers (open-coat paper clogs less) for flats. He folds half sheets of sandpaper in thirds so that the grit-coated faces don't abrade each other, a trick that can make papers last considerably longer.

1

2

3

[hvlpsprayers]

SPRAY-PAINTING USUALLY prompts images of pressurized cans with cheap plastic valves and noxious fumes, or paint-encrusted auto-body guys generating fog banks of colored mist. Spray-painting a mailbox isn't quite like doing up a Lincoln, but the two systems are surprisingly similar. Both harness compressed air to atomize paint and create a thin, even film unblemished by brush marks. "Problem is," says painting contractor John Dee, "you'd better mask, move or cover anything that's nearby, because most of the paint will be lost."

That's why, when it comes to putting a slick finish on cabinets or woodwork, Dee uses a high-volume, low-pressure (HVLP) spray-painting system.

Unlike compressor-based systems that move up to 15 cubic feet of air per minute at pressures of up to 175 pounds per square inch, an HVLP system uses a turbine that can push as much as 100 cfm at less than 10 psi. Finely machined HVLP spray guns focus the turbine-generated air into the paint stream, creating a fine mist of slow-moving droplets. Up to 90 percent of the paint from an HVLP sprayer lands on target, compared with 35 percent or less for conventional, compressor-powered systems. Paint that doesn't land where it's supposed to is more than a nuisance, however. Overspray affects air quality and wallets: Some of Dee's paint costs $110 a gallon.

For work outdoors, an HVLP sprayer is at a disadvantage. It's slow, and the slightest breeze wafts the spray away. On the other hand, "When I have to paint tricky stuff like steam radiators and louvered shutters," Dee says, "it's great." If you've ever brush-painted shutters, you'll know exactly what he means. And if the wind is calm, an HVLP sprayer can make relatively short work of painting the diagonal slats of wood-lattice panels shielding the underpinnings of decks and porches.

Dee's deluxe HVLP system features a 2.5-gallon pressure pot (the blue cylinder atop the turbine) big enough to hold an open can of paint. This option increases capacity, reduces cleanup and refill time and lightens the spray gun—an important consideration when spraying overhead.

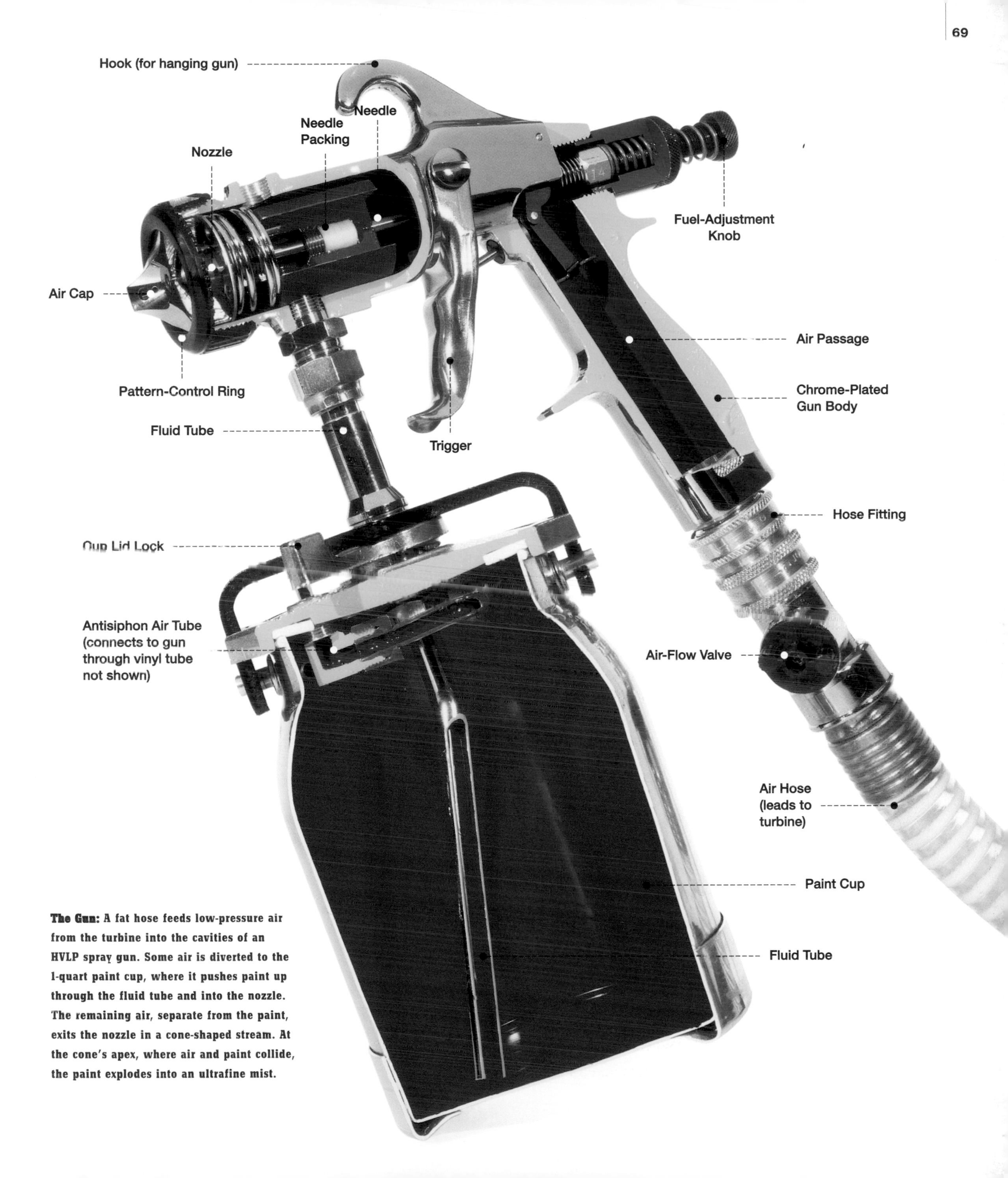

The Gun: A fat hose feeds low-pressure air from the turbine into the cavities of an HVLP spray gun. Some air is diverted to the 1-quart paint cup, where it pushes paint up through the fluid tube and into the nozzle. The remaining air, separate from the paint, exits the nozzle in a cone-shaped stream. At the cone's apex, where air and paint collide, the paint explodes into an ultrafine mist.

[hvlpsprayers]

Setting up the sprayer is no big deal. Dee hooks up and unkinks the hose, then pours paint or primer into the paint cup through a mesh strainer to catch clumps and impurities. Latex paint can be sprayed without thinning, but Dee usually adds a thinner that maintains the paint's body. He thins alkyds (oil-based paints) with naphtha because it evaporates faster than thinners made with mineral spirits. Despite dramatic reductions in overspray, however, Dee always works with a respirator or air-supplied hood to keep paint out of his nose and lungs. A swab of petroleum jelly on any exposed facial skin, especially eyelids, makes cleanup easier. And he still masks off areas adjacent to his work—to reduce the chances of a "direct hit," he says.

Dee always has his gun hand in motion, even before he starts spraying, and his hand continues moving after he releases the trigger. Stopping even momentarily increases the chance of runs or sags. He makes long, parallel passes as he sprays, keeping the gun the same distance from the work at all times. Watching him work, it's easy to see how the quickness and precision of the sprayer makes short work of big jobs. But HVLP sprayers aren't just for painting cabinets and cars. You'll find them also in tire plants (to spray release agents into tire molds) and in shoe factories (to spray tanning chemicals onto leather). Ever wonder how the sugar coating gets on fortune cookies? Yep, HVLP again.

TECHNIQUES

Painting Cabinets: After removing and sanding cabinet doors, Dee lays each one flat, "boxing" the spraying by sweeping lengthwise, then widthwise. Doors get four coats.

Painting Shutters: Painting shutters or louvered doors is a project that cries out for HVLP. Dee first sprays the end grain of the louvers and the back of the control rod, then hits the inside edges of the stiles as he moves the louvers up and down. This is no job for a brush, he says.

Painting Trim: With skin, lungs and ceiling protected, Dee can spray-paint crown moldings with ease. For fine work, he restricts paint flow, turning the sprayer into a tool that can rival the pinpoint precision of an artist's airbrush.

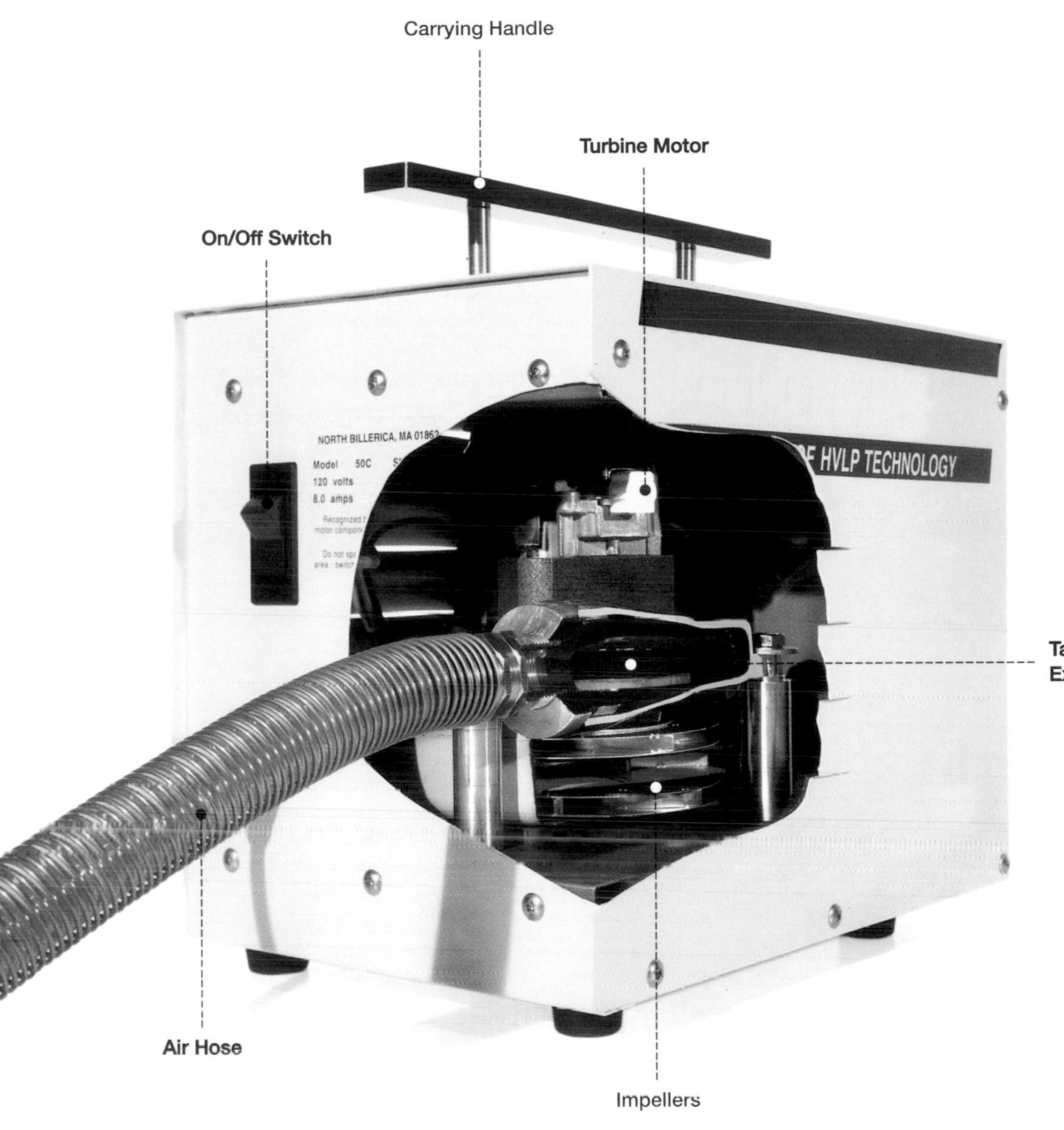

The Turbine: Like a vacuum cleaner running in reverse, an HVLP turbine delivers a lot of air at low pressure as soon as you turn it on. (Compressor-driven sprayers must build up air-tank pressure first.) Turbines come with 2- or 3-stage impellers, or fans. Three-stage models generate more pressure and move thicker paint. Two air filters on this turbine prevent dust from being sucked in and mixing with the paint. Solvents sucked into the turbine may cause an explosion, so for safety, the turbine should be kept 20 feet away from the gun.

spray patterns

ROUND: Round patterns work well in tight spots but increase the risk of sags and drips because they concentrate the paint into a small area.

OVAL: Horizontal ovals are best when moving the gun up and down. A gun's spray pattern can be adjusted easily by turning the air cap.

OVAL: Vertical ovals give the most coverage when moving the gun sideways. If the shape isn't symmetrical, the paint nozzle or air passages might be dirty.

[exterior painting]

"SOME boards gleamed, BUT AFTER JUST THREE YEARS OUTSIDE, OTHERS WERE ALMOST BARE— A SIGN THAT SOMEONE CUT corners by using CHEAP ingredients."

[paintproblems]

PAINTER JOHN DEE calls his neighbors "the epitome of diligent homeowners." They bought a postwar Colonial, and a month later Andrea was down at the local hardware store, picking out new beige paint to lighten up the gloomy exterior. Soon Robert was up on the ladder, hard at work. "It wasn't easy," he says. "I scraped the whole house, rented a water gun, primed everything. I put two coats of paint over that. I did it when I got home from work, I did it on Saturdays. It took me the whole summer. It looked so good."

a bulge *or paint flakes at the top of a wall suggest problems caused by gutter or roof leaks. Find and fix the problems before you paint the wall, or else paint won't last long in this area.*

But within a year, as the couple watched in horror, their labor-intensive paint job—and everything underneath—was flaking off in leathery sheets. The paint detached with such determination that some chips were embedded with cedar splinters from the underlying siding. Layers of paint that had bonded to the house for decades came loose.

"You can generally tell if you have a house that is going to peel if you probe around a bit," Dee says. "But my neighbors had no previous paint problems, and they went by the book." Dee has understandable sympathy for the two: Not long after his own rented house was repainted, it began peeling so badly the south wall looked like a head of hair after a botched perm. "It's a total blowout," he says.

About one in ten paint jobs goes awry, says David Chupka, a technical manager for the Sherwin Williams Co. Often it's because of cutting corners—not sanding, not scrubbing, painting just before a storm, ignoring long-term moisture penetration. But people who own old homes can do everything they're told by paint salesmen and follow labels devotedly and still wind up with paint that peels. If they've hired someone to do the work, at prices that can rival the cost of a new car, peeling paint can begin to look like dollar bills floating off with each breeze.

William C. Feist thinks he knows why. The problem can occur when an old house with layers of oil-base paint is coated with a water-base paint, says Feist, who headed the federal government's house-paint research program for 20 years. "The homeowners decide to upgrade and put on good latex paint. But that last coat of a new type of paint can be sufficient to cause a catastrophic failure, often right down to bare wood."

When people in the paint industry have a problem, they often consult with the chemical company that supplies them with the ingredients they put in their cans. In the United States, almost all paint companies turn to Rohm & Haas and its Paint Quality Institute in Spring House, Pennsylvania, near Philadelphia. There, in a six-acre field draped

Trying to figure out what paint to use on a new house—or how to remedy paint problems on an old house—is exasperating. One remedy comes from knowing that latex paints and oil paints cure very differently.

[paintproblems]

with two miles of odd-looking fences, 25,000 paint samples are in a contest with time, weather and the sun. On a blustery day one winter, the institute's technical director, Walter J. Gozdan, led the way through this maze, happy to talk about what people in the paint business like to call coatings.

Essentially, he said, there are two kinds of house paint: oil (also called alkyd because of the alcohols and acids used to make a synthetic oil) and so-called latex (which, it turns out, has no rubber in it). Both consist of three main components: a pigment, a binder that glues the pigment to a surface as the paint dries and a solvent that makes the mixture loose enough to brush on.

Oil paint forms a tough, plastic film as the binder reacts with oxygen in the air. The binder can be a natural oil, such as linseed squeezed out of flaxseed, or oil modified with alkyds. Latex paint, however, forms a flexible film as water evaporates and the once-floating spheres of binder and pigment move closer together and fuse. Latex paint was invented at the end of World War II using synthetic rubber as the binder. Today the binder is most often a pure acrylic, a vinyl-acrylic or a vinyl-acetate.

What might look like paint failure could instead be a failure of the underlying material. A new coat of paint, for example, would hardly help these decayed cedar shingles.

The critical difference between oil and latex paints is that they do not cure in the same way. Oil paint never stops curing. As it ages, it continues to oxidize, becoming more and more brittle. Latex cures in about two weeks and stays pliable. Oil paint generally adheres better to problem surfaces because the oils are small enough to seep into the wood or microscopic openings in old paint. The resins in latex paint are generally too big to seep into anything. But that can be advantageous. The gaps between the larger particles in latex paint allow water vapor to pass through. This makes latex less likely to peel from homes with excessive interior moisture.

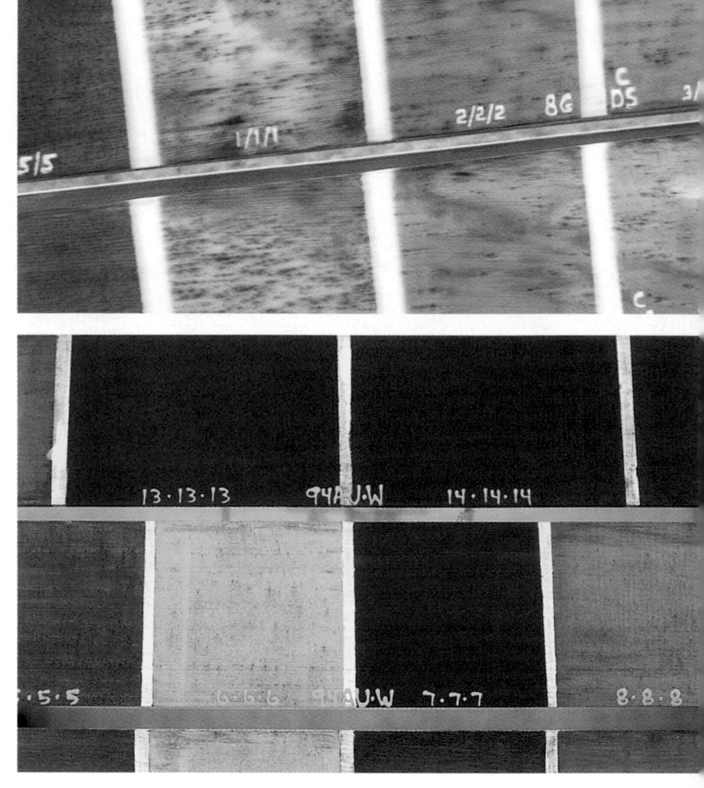

What the research reveals: Clear finishes (top) are short-lived outdoors because sunlight gets through the finish to break down wood fibers. Earth-toned paints (above) outlast bright colors because they don't break down in sunlight.

As Gozdan paused near the middle of the paint maze, he pointed out how all this theory translates into reality. At a series of mock-ups of window frames coated with oil paint, he jabbed a finger at stringy hairline cracks on some of the wood and deeper, squarish cracks on others. Both, he said, are evidence that the

When moisture gets behind siding or trim, it can literally push paint off the front. If an entire wall is peeling, that may mean that moisture vapor is moving through the walls and is being drawn through the wood when sunshine warms the wall. If window trim alone is peeling, pry off trim boards and plug gaps around the frame with a low-expansion foam sealant.

[paint problems]

oil paint had become too brittle to keep up with the expansion and contraction of the wood. Then Gozdan walked to a nearby section where dozens of three-foot-long pine boards were painted with white latex from a variety of manufacturers. Some boards gleamed, but after just three years outside, others were almost bare—a sign, he said, that someone cut corners by using cheap ingredients. The lessons here are that latex outperforms oil and that expensive all-acrylic latex works better than less expensive latex with vinyl-acrylics.

Rohm & Haas has a vested interest in this position: Paint gave it a postwar market for acrylics, which had been going by the ton into Plexiglas airplane windows. Still, one of the few independent paint research centers in the country, the U.S. government's Forest Products Laboratory in Madison, Wisconsin, agrees. The lab compared oil and latex paints on its own test fences strung across a windy hillside. "We have twenty-year-old latex that looks as good as if it were new," says chemist Mark T. Knaebe. The side of a typical house, he says, should get more protection from two coats of latex over a primer coat than it would from two coats of a modern oil paint over a primer.

No wonder paint salespeople tout the benefits of latex. But what many don't realize is that all the tests that find latex to be superior have been done by painting over bare wood clapboards or over wood that had only one or two coats of old paint. No one has tested what works best over many layers of old paint. Most houses built before 1950, as well as many newer ones, are covered with multiple layers of oil paint.

When Gozdan is asked how this might affect the institute's recommendations, his answer is surprising: "I would never use latex over multiple coats of oil paint. You stand a

six signs of paint failure

ALLIGATORING
Causes: Natural aging of oil paint; undercoat was wet; or top coat is harder than the base (such as alkyd enamel over latex).
Remedy: Strip to bare wood, prime and paint.

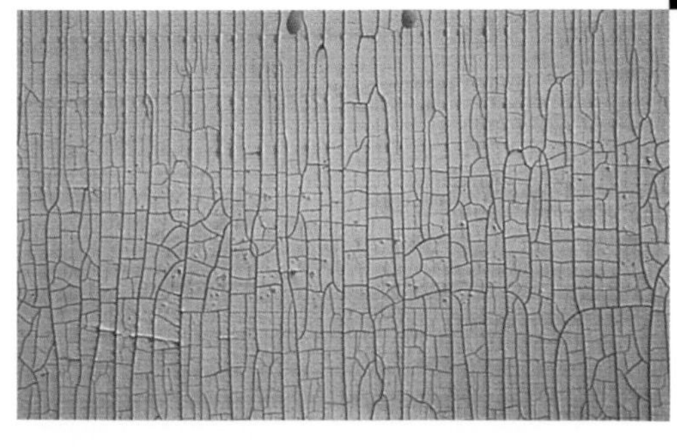

INCOMPATIBILITY
Causes: Use of latex over more than three or four layers of oil paint.
Remedy: Strip to bare wood. Or scrape, prime and repaint with latex—but expect unscraped parts to peel later.

BLISTERING
Causes: Wall painted while in sun; wall has moisture problem; surface was damp (for oil paint) or humidity was high (latex).
Remedy: If blisters go down to wood, fix the moisture problem. Scrape, spot-prime, repaint in shade.

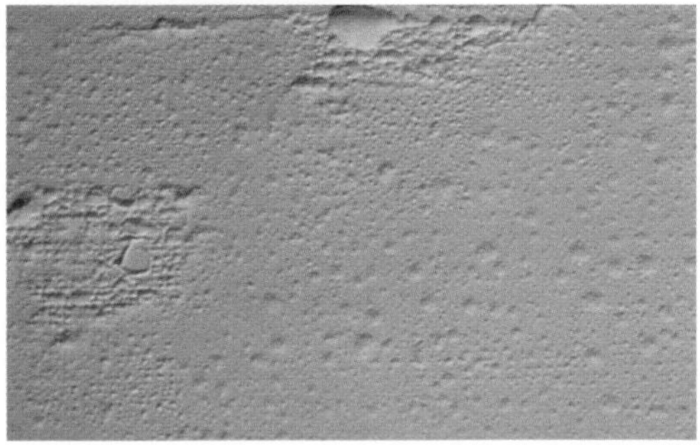

chance of peeling off all the paint if you switch." Latex paint can literally pull old oil paint off the house, he says. "I've seen houses where the paint has come off in four-by-eight-foot sheets."

When a flexible layer of latex bonds on top of brittle oil paint, the old paint becomes a thin rope in a tug-of-war. As sunshine hits the wall, the wood and the latex can expand. But the oil paint in the middle is brittle, and either cracks or loosens its grip on the wood underneath. "The latex tends to accelerate the paint loss," says Carl Minchew, director of technical services for Benjamin Moore & Co.

Gary Barrett, director of technical services for the Painting & Decorating Contractors of America, says the stress on the old oil paint is greatest during the few weeks it takes latex to cure, although the results may take months or years to become fully evident. "It's the shrink factor of latex,"

If paint looks bubbly or loose near the bottom of a wall or trim piece, rot caused by splashing water or ground contact may be the culprit, as Tom Silva shows. The bottom edge of siding and trim should be at least 8 inches from earth.

Barrett says. "It has to coalesce, or it can't cure."

The force of this effect varies. Often, houses with layers of old oil paint can be successfully covered with modern latex. But when it doesn't work, the results may be disastrous. "It's very unpredictable," says John G. Stauffer, director of

PEELING
Causes: Moisture in wall; poor surface preparation; low-quality paint; surface was wet (oil paint only) or blistered.
Remedy: Fix moisture problem, scrape and sand.

CRACKING/FLAKING
Causes: Low quality or excessively thinned paint; poor surface preparation or lack of primer; latex dried too fast because temperature was too cool or wind too high.
Remedy: If cracks are on surface layer alone, scrape and sand, then prime and repaint; otherwise strip to bare wood.

WRINKLING
Causes: Paint was too thick; surface or weather was too hot; uncured paint got wet or humidity rose; undercoat was dirty.
Remedy: Scrape or sand to remove wrinkles. In hot or damp weather, wait longer to recoat.

[preparingwindows]

COMPARED TO THE VISUAL APPEAL OF A WELL-MAINTAINED OLD wood window, most modern, "low-maintenance" windows fall far short. Yet in our eagerness to lower heating bills and live in draft-free comfort (or, perhaps, to avoid scraping windows caked with old paint), we readily consign old windows to the dump. At one *This Old House* project (in Salem, Massachusetts), the home inspector sized up the windows as being "past their useful life." But Norm Abram was convinced they should be saved.

Replacing missing glazing compound is critical care for old windows. Ignoring this step and simply painting over the damage is a shortcut you'll regret once the windows leak.

"The old sash on this house are amazing," he said. "Just look at the condition of the wood. After 230 years, it's still in great shape." But the long-neglected windows looked pretty bad. Peeling paint indicated that water was getting in behind the glazing compound that held the glass in place. On some panes, the putty had cracked and curled; even where the putty looked good, Norm could slip his knife blade between putty and glass. Faced with a similar situation, many a homeowner has simply painted over the damage and hoped for the best. That's shortsighted, however, because the timely replacement of bad putty can save an entire sash from eventual destruction.

Of the three components in a window sash—the wood, the glass and the glazing compound—the compound is the weakest link. Glazing compound (or putty) closes the gap between wood and glass, sloping ever so slightly to direct water away from the wood. But because one of putty's major ingredients, linseed oil, evaporates over time, the putty eventually dries out and shrinks away from the glass, letting moisture seep in to peel off paint or rot wood.

Norm has repaired many windows over the years, and once as a youngster even reglazed and reputtied the windows of his grandmother's boardinghouse. He has strong memories of those summer days and the tangy smell of linseed putty on his hands. His most important discovery about the work: "There are no shortcuts. You have to take your time." Glazing compound manufacturers—as well as some painters—recommend stripping out good putty with bad because old putty can leach oil from new. Others figure it's better to patch the damage than put off the job, particularly because often the only areas that have to be re-puttied are the lower horizontal surfaces where water tends to collect. Norm, however, doesn't patch putty. "The old compound is bound to fail sooner than the new stuff; better to have it all be the same age instead of trying to make a patch." If that means removing the sash from

SASH: The framework that holds the glass. Consists of stiles (vertical members), rails (horizontal members) and muntins. Most sash in the U.S. is either single- or double-hung (slides up and down in a jamb) or casement (side-hung on hinges).

MUNTINS: Narrow strips of wood that support the glass panes within a sash. Do not confuse with mullions—those are vertical elements that separate side-by-side windows.

FRAME: The wooden structure that houses and supports the sash.

JAMB: The vertical part of the frame within which the sash slides or rests.

PANE: The glass or glazing in the sash. Sometimes called a light.

SILL: The lower exterior member of a window frame, sloped outward to shed water.

A Window Lexicon: To a window expert, the Federal-style windows on this old house would be described as "plank-frame with single-hung, six-over-six plain-rail sash." Translation: A plank-frame is a window frame made of thick wood members pegged together and nailed to the wood sheathing. Single-hung means that only the bottom sash moves. Six-over-six refers to the six panes of glass in each sash. Plain-rail refers to sash that slide directly against each other instead of in separate tracks.

[preparing windows]

the window, so be it. Replacing putty doesn't always call for the complete removal of the sash, however. If the windows are in fairly good shape, you can simply rake out the old putty (see page 86) and press in new putty without disturbing the window. In any case, a reglazed window, properly maintained, should last 20 years before the job has to be repeated.

to make sure
that new putty doesn't peek above the muntins, putty one side of the window and then look through from the other side. Scrape off any excess putty before it dries.

REBUILDING A WINDOW

When windows are in need of major repairs, as were those on the Salem House, Norm first removes the sash by taking out the stops (the vertical pieces of wood that confine the sash within the jamb). For stops nailed to the jamb, it's a simple matter to slip in a putty knife and gently pry the stop free, working from the bottom up. Sometimes the sash has been painted and caulked shut. That's when Norm reaches for a carbide-tipped scraper and a thin putty knife, and removes the caulk and cracks the paint film from around the perimeter of the sash to free it. Once the sash is free, Norm reworks it on a table whenever possible. "It's easier, and I'm less likely to damage the glass."

PUTTYING A WINDOW

When sash repairs are complete and the glass is in place, it's putty time. From this point on, the steps are identical to those used to putty windows without first removing them.

"Now comes the trickiest part," says Norm: "Tooling the putty." This part of the

repairing sash and replacing putty

Sand the sash: After removing the sash for rehabilitation, Norm places it on a table and puts his belt sander to work removing old paint and smoothing the stiles and rails (below). He steers clear of the muntins, however, because a belt sander can quickly destroy this delicate woodwork. A disposable respirator for Norm and a vacuum attachment (with HEPA filter) for the sander minimize exposure to lead dust or to the asbestos that was used in glazing compound manufactured before 1977.

Sand again: After removing the glass, Norm removes glazing points and stray bits of putty, then sands the wood gently with an in-line detail sander.

Scrape: Using a well-sharpened paint scraper, Norm scrapes paint from the top edge of the muntins, which makes it easier to distinguish wood from putty as the putty is chipped out. Removing putty with a putty knife requires care and concentration.

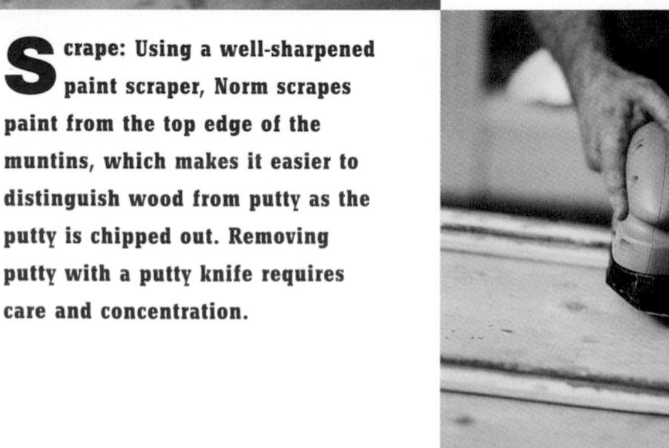

job is common to every window reputtying project. With his thumb, Norm presses a thick layer of putty against the rabbet and around the edge of the glass. Starting at one corner, he pulls the putty knife over the glazing compound in one firm stroke. To maintain a consistent angle, he keeps one corner of the knife on the glass, in line with the edge of the rabbet, and rests the end of the blade on the wood. If the knife pulls out the putty, either the knife is dirty or the putty needs warming; remove the putty and try again. With practice, you can put a neat crease in the corner with a single stroke. "The less you play with it, the better," says Norm. At this stage, obsessive smoothing can undo a perfectly adequate job.

Norm uses a hand-warmed wad of putty to pick up the excess left on the glass without denting the beveled putty. On the inside of the window, he trims away any squeeze-out between glass and muntin with his putty knife. Then he reinstalls the sash in the frame and replaces the stops.

Depending on humidity, the glazing compound will cure in two to three weeks. Oil paint can be applied the next day, however (latex paint won't adhere until the glazing compound has cured). Putty is ready for paint if it feels like a fresh cookie: a bit soft on the inside but crisp on the outside, so that lightly pressing a finger doesn't leave an imprint. The last step: Norm tells the painter to make sure that the edge of the paint overlaps the glass slightly, providing an added barrier against water infiltration. And in case you're wondering, professionals never mask the glass before painting. Even for novices, it usually takes less time to paint carefully and scrape off any excess than it would to tape off the glass.

Prime: Norm paints an oil-based primer over all wood surfaces. Priming the rabbets protects the wood, but also keeps oil from leaching out of the glazing compound.

Putty: After the primer dries, Norm presses a bead of compound onto the rabbet (below), and then wiggles each pane into the putty. No portion of the glass should touch wood.

Point: Using his putty knife, Norm gently slides new metal glazing points across the glass and presses each one halfway into the wood. Even small panes get at keast six points: two on each side, and one each at top and bottom.

Putty again: Norm kneads a wad of putty (making it tacky and elastic), thumbs it into place and then forces it flat with deft passes of his putty knife.

[putty buddies]

THERE ARE ALL SORTS OF ways to remove those fossilized chunks of glazing compound that cling, albeit precariously, to window muntins. The worst portions practically fall off at first touch, but most must be coaxed off by more concerted efforts. Some window repair experts prefer to use hand tools and a heat gun, while others (including Norm Abram) prefer a stiff putty knife and plenty of patience. Depending on how much work there is to do, various power tools may even be appropriate. Here are your options.

to avoid *overheating and possibly cracking panes when removing putty with a heat gun, cover the glass with an aluminum plate.*

A leather-handled wedge is simple, effective and doesn't make much dust. It has a 5-inch chisel-shaped blade for digging out the loose putty without damaging the wood. Just line it up with the putty and tap it—gently.

One brand of detail sander can be fitted with a blade that removes the glazing compound without scratching the glass. The oscillating blade makes a lot of noise, however, and the tool takes some time to get used to. To avoid grinding into wood, stick a piece of masking tape on the blade as a depth guide. The tool isn't advised for use on putties made before 1970, which often contain asbestos, or for windows that may contain lead paint. (For more on detail sanders, see page 12.)

One putty scrambler chucks into an electric drill. It pulverizes putty but requires great control to avoid gouging the wood, particularly fragile muntins. For best results, make a shallow pass first, then adjust the bit to make a slightly deeper swipe.

Some craftsmen soften glazing compound with a heat gun and peel it off with a putty blade. Norm, however, suggests caution when using a heat gun. "When there's lead paint," he says, "heat guns generate toxic fumes, and there's a greater likelihood of burning the wood or breaking the glass." Indeed, every method has its trade-offs. A blowtorch, although expeditious, can singe wood and break glass; a heat gun with a special nozzle may offer more control but takes longer.

TECHNIQUES

Wedge and hammer: Removing putty by gradually coaxing it away from the sash with the aid of a hammer tap (1) is a low-tech option that is easy to control.

Oscillating blade: A detail sander (2) works by wiggling its sanding pad back and forth at high speed. The same action can part putty from its bed if the pad is swapped for a blade, but not all sanders will accept such specialty slicers.

Drill attachment: An electric drill fitted with a rotary attachment (3) chews through putty; this pairing is less convenient to use if the sash is two stories up a ladder.

Heat gun and blade: Heated putty (4) peels off wood smoothly, but the risk of releasing toxic lead fumes limits this technique to well-ventilated areas.

[damagedwood]

THE WAND-SHAPED grinder bites deep into a stile at the bottom of the garage door. Plowing like a DDS through dentin, John Stahl grimaces slightly as the tool chews through punky wood with a stinging whine. After a couple of minutes, he eases back on the trigger and surveys the cavity he has made. "You'd think your dentist was nuts if he didn't get out all the decay, right?" he says. "It's the same with rot. I don't stop until I get down to good wood. I know when I hit it by the sound of the cutter. It changes to a high *wreeee*." Stahl repairs rot, but it's much easier, he says, to stop it before it starts.

when working *with epoxy wood fillers, apply them sparingly to minimize the need for sanding later on—epoxy is tough stuff.*

"You'll get rot wherever wood never completely dries out," he says, eyeing the garage door. The relentless, voracious fungi that feast on wood thrive in such moist conditions. Windowsills with cracked paint and open joints, the end grain of an exposed rafter... these are places where fungi, aided by oxygen and warm air, routinely take hold and do immense, expensive damage.

When he finds rot, Stahl aims to fix the problem without destroying the detail. "In an older house, the wood is almost always better than anything you can buy to replace it. When people say to me, 'Why are you going to this trouble? Just rip it out!' I tell them it's like driving a Rolls-Royce with a bad paint job and bald tires. Why trade it in for a Yugo?"

Rot in structural members calls for special care. This hastily repaired post should have been entirely replaced.

Specialists who regularly use rot-repair products differ on which technique works best. One camp believes in restoring the damaged wood's strength by infusing it with a thin liquid epoxy called a consolidant. Stahl, however, doubts the durability of that approach and works out of the other camp: Eliminate the soft stuff, add some borate and use a thick epoxy paste to fill the cavity. After getting the rot out, Stahl drills 5⁄16-inch holes in the solid wood and fills them with borate gel and pellets. The fluoride of wood rot repair, borate compound helps prevent damage if the wood gets moist again. Moisture makes the borate diffuse into the wood and kill fungi.

Stahl next brushes the excavated area with

Good paint often hides bad wood, and the only way to find rot is to probe suspect spots with a knife or awl. Damage is revealed by the tool's easy penetration. Stahl also checks suspect areas with a moisture meter. A reading higher than 18 percent is a clear signal that the wood is rotting.

[damagedwood]

a low-viscosity epoxy to strengthen the bond between the good wood and the patching compound. Then he pulls out an epoxy injector that carries tubes of resin and hardener that make up the two-part epoxy he uses. When he squeezes the trigger, they merge on their way through a 6-inch mixing tip and flow into the cavity. On a cool day, Stahl has about an hour to sculpt the epoxy with his putty knife. When he needs to form a long, straight edge and a flat surface, however, Stahl sometimes uses a strip of Plexiglas, which doesn't bond with epoxy, as a casting mold.

Moisture can hasten a repair failure if the wood gets wet enough to swell and break its seal with the epoxy. Once rot is removed, however, the surrounding wood quickly returns to a relatively dry state (10 to 15 percent moisture content). In high humidity conditions (say, July in New Orleans), Stahl might use a heat gun to speed the drying.

The wood should also be kept relatively dry post-repair to avoid creating an environment that would encourage the growth of fungi. Stahl's epoxy will take just one day to cure enough to allow a few passes with a belt sander to take off its almost glassy slickness and make it dead level with the adjacent wood. A couple of coats of paint will provide the necessary protection from ultraviolet rays and make the patch almost invisible.

Stahl steps back to admire his work. It took a little more than an hour to undo damage that was more than 30 years in the making. "Only a fungus would know that isn't real wood," he says with a chuckle.

TECHNIQUES

Preparing: Painter John Dee's approach to rot-repair is similar to Stahl's. After removing sections of rotted wood from this porch column, he brushed on a runny epoxy that penetrated the wood and ensured a good bond with the thicker epoxy filler to follow.

Mixing: After the epoxy primer had set (in about 20 minutes), Dee mixed a thick, sag-resistant epoxy that would cling to the vertical surfaces. Some epoxies run slightly before they start to harden and must be held in place with plastic-lined forms.

Filling: After laying down plastic film to protect the granite stoop, Dee pushed epoxy into all the voids. On this hot day, he had to do all the shaping within five minutes using disposable putty knives. After the epoxy cured, he shaped it.

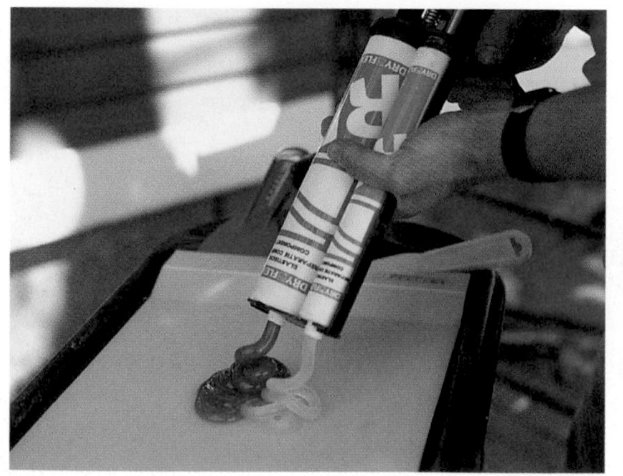

Rot fungi steal wood's strength and weight, leaving nothing but a fluffy pulp. This handful of decay was an exterior windowsill before portions were excavated prior to an epoxy repair. The decision to undertake extensive repairs or simply to replace the rotted wood is often a judgement call based on experience.

[housewashing]

WITH NO SHORTAGE of ways to pass a sunny fall day, it might seem absurd to spend time on paint that's in pretty good shape. But a day's work now could add years to the life of your paint—and keep thousands of dollars in your pocket. "The most important thing homeowners can do to protect their paint is to hose down their walls once a year," says painter Seth Knipe, who worked on the *This Old House* dream house in Milton, Massachusetts. Washing not only removes dirt and keeps paint looking good, but it also exposes spots on siding and trim that should be touched up with primer and paint, thus forestalling the necessity of a major repainting.

Before the wash-down, walk around the house and look for anything that can hold water against wood. Leaves and dirt can build up around the foundation, and both can ruin paint and eventually rot wood. Aim for at least 8 inches of clearance between wood and earth, but not if it means digging a moat around the house. Also, prune shrubs and trees so they don't touch walls. "Without air flow, even a heavy dew may keep the walls moist," Knipe says. Mildew flourishes on moist paint.

When you're ready to wash the walls, use a garden hose with a standard nozzle. And as you wield the hose, inspect the paint. "Check the windowsills, the corner boards, around the garage doors," Knipe says. "Those are usually the first areas to peel." If the siding has black splotches, test for mildew by dabbing suspect surfaces with household bleach: Dirt won't fade, but mildew will. To kill this fungus and reduce the chance that it will grow back, squirt the wall with a wood cleaner or bleach solution (one pint of household bleach to one gallon of water). Wait 10 minutes, then rinse thoroughly. Stubborn stains can be scrubbed with a stiff brush. If mildew is widespread, however, pressure washing (see page 94) is probably a better strategy.

After the washing is done, be patient—you can't necessarily wash in the morning and paint in the afternoon. It could take as much as a week for the walls to dry thoroughly. But when they do, scrape off any peeling patches, sand them to smooth the junction with sound paint, spot-prime and touch up with fresh paint. After two or three years, what's on the house may have faded, and the touched-up spots will look glossier. "There's not a lot you can do about that," Knipe says, "but it does keep the paint from getting worse."

House paint benefits from regular grime removal. Spraying the siding periodically also pinpoints trouble spots.

[pressurewashers]

AMAZING STUFF, water. As it sprays from a sprinkler at 40 pounds per square inch, water is a benign plaything for squealing children. But fed through the pinhole nozzle of a painter's pressure washer at up to 4,000 psi, the incompressible liquid becomes as unyielding as Swedish steel: hard enough to carve divots in wood, blast mortar from brickwork or even slice off a hand.

Throttled back and aimed with care, though, a pressure washer makes quick work of dirty jobs, such as prepping a house for painting. Ever wonder how new cars look so clean on the lot? Dealers spray them with non-spotting, deionized water from a pressure washer. But cleaning houses is how pressure washers earn their keep. That's what pro Bill Darlington does most days on homes throughout the Philadelphia suburbs. His van-mounted pressure washer, a muscular version of the washer painters use, keeps running spring, summer and fall, blasting moss off patios, soot off stone and algae off decks. Scampering up an extension ladder at one job, Darlington swipes his hand across the side of a seemingly white gutter to show how filthy it really is. Like flypaper, gutters collect all sorts of airborne junk. "Diesel smoke," he says, "that's the worst." Back on terra firma, Darlington rigs his washer for battle. Grabbing a clear plastic siphon tube that branches off the washer's spray hose, he sticks it into a bucket of detergent. The tube will suck solution out of the bucket and draw it into the hose whenever he pulls the trigger on the washer's spray wand. When Darlington trains a spray of soapy water on the gutters, grime dissolves.

This ability to deliver chemicals and water under high pressure makes the pressure washer a favored weapon in the fight against mildew, the black mold that stains houses in some parts of the country and drives painters wild. "If you paint over mildew," warns Darlington, "it'll grow right through the paint film and you'll never get rid of it." Sodium hypochlorite, the active ingredient in bleach, kills mildew and its spores on contact; mixed with water and forced into the wood's surface under pressure, bleach seeks out and destroys even the sneakiest spores. Painters, particularly in New England, often assume that pressure washing is part of the paint job and bid accordingly. If you're doing the washing instead, coordinate your efforts with the painter. Walls can't be painted too soon after washing, but if you wait too long, mildew will seize the opportunity and reestablish itself.

And as any painter worth his brushes will tell you, don't rely on pressure washing to save

Electric pressure washers are easier to care for, more portable and quieter than gas-engine washers. But they top out at about 1,800 psi, and must be plugged into a GFCI (ground fault circuit interrupter).

The 5½ hp engine of this pressure-washing brute pumps up to 3 gallons per minute at 2,000 psi. Four-cycle engines like this call for the same care as a lawn mower: Change dirty oil and filters, pop in a new spark plug yearly and add fuel stabilizer if gas sits in the tank.

[pressure washers]

yourself from scraping paint. Sure, the water blasts off the loosest stuff (and sprinkles potentially lead-laced debris all over your yard), but it won't get the rest.

Pressure-washing a house is a workout that calls for a methodical approach. Starting at the bottom of a wall, Darlington sprays the bleach and water solution at low pressure, sweeping back and forth with overlapping passes until he reaches the top. Switching to a soap solution, he repeats the process to loosen dirt, chalk and bleach, then makes a third pass with clear water at high pressure, working from the top down. To prevent bleach and detergent from drying, he rinses each wall thoroughly before moving to the next. There's no such thing as rinsing a bleached house too much. If residue remains, it will weaken the new paint's bond and corrode metal.

Any time wood shingles and clapboard are sprayed, a cautious, test-and-see approach is best. Too much pressure can plow furrows in wood, and spraying upward at too low an angle will inject water and chemicals behind the siding. Done right, the house will be dry enough to paint in a couple of days. Done wrong, it may take weeks to recover.

There are three ways to control a washer's power. One is with engine speed. Darlington's pump can move four gallons per minute at 4,000 psi, but most days he throttles back to 2,800 psi. Even at that pressure, the hose turns rock-hard, and the wand has a noticeable kick when it sprays. Spray tips provide a finer measure of control. Darlington carries an assortment in his pocket and swaps them for different situations. The basic tips are classified by their spray width: 40-, 25-, 15- and 0-degree. The 40 tip produces a soft, flat fan ideal for rinsing; a 0 tip focuses water into a narrow, piercing stream that can obliterate stains from stone or reach up to gables. Darlington's workhorses are the low-pressure 15-degree and high-pressure 25-degree tips.

The third control is distance. Water's velocity (and its power) drops rapidly after exiting a nozzle. Darlington is careful to hold the nozzle a uniform distance from whatever surface he's working on, so that no part of the house is cleaner than another.

When buying or renting a washer, pressure is a key feature to consider, but it isn't the only one. Pressure and water flow have to be kept in balance or cleaning power suffers.

SIPHON: This hose enables a pressure washer to suck water out of a wet basement.

ADJUST: One adjustable tip delivers an array of spray widths and two pressure settings.

ROTATE: A special nozzle that spins easily strips paint from masonry.

BLAST: Basic washing tips are classified by the spread of their spray. Colored collars make them easy to identify.

Bleach and detergent greatly augment a pressure washer's cleaning power. Darlington's machine can suck the solutions from buckets directly into the spray hose.

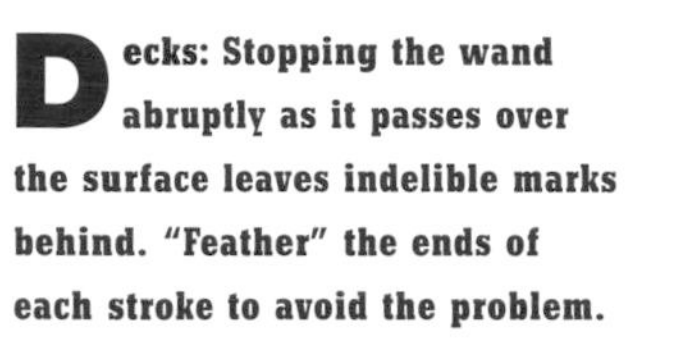

Decks: Stopping the wand abruptly as it passes over the surface leaves indelible marks behind. "Feather" the ends of each stroke to avoid the problem.

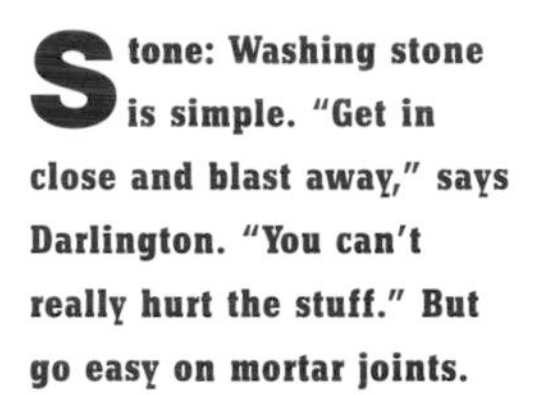

Stone: Washing stone is simple. "Get in close and blast away," says Darlington. "You can't really hurt the stuff." But go easy on mortar joints.

New wood: A washer with a high-pressure tip does more than raise grain; it will blow craters in wood. To prove it, Darlington blasted a scrap of decking (above) for only a few seconds before it splintered.

Siding: A 25-degree tip wipes algae off shingles. Spraying a house demands care because of the washer's ability to inject water behind siding. Never spray electrical wires—electricity can follow a water stream back to the sprayer.

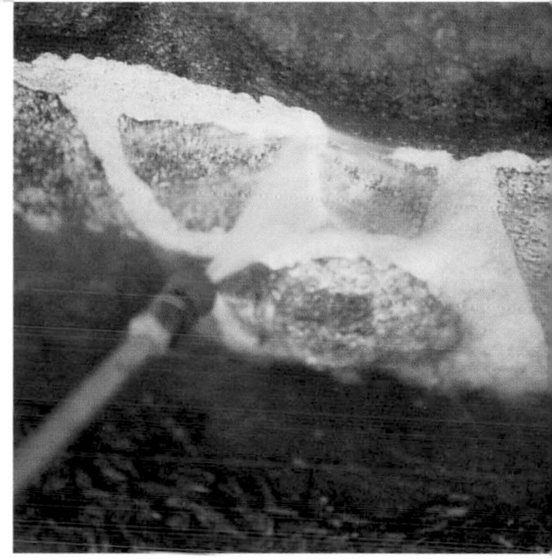

According to Dick Darlington, Bill's older brother and the other half of Darlington Restoration, a good machine for homeowners would deliver between 3 and 4 gpm at 1,500 to 2,000 psi. If you're buying a washer, he recommends getting one that has a good engine, with durable cast-iron cylinder sleeves or a reputation for easy starting. He wouldn't use a machine that circulates chemicals through the pump; bleach and detergent shorten piston and valve life. Washers with downstream injectors are a better choice because they introduce chemicals to the water that has already passed through the pump. Pressure washers that meet Dick Darlington's criteria have gas engines, not electric motors. Higher pressures and bigger flows calls for a bigger engine, a change that can boost the cost of a pressure washer considerably.

After a day on the job, a wet, worn-out Darlington is dirty enough to need pressure washing himself. He's smart enough to know better—even the least powerful tips could force bleach-laden water through his skin and into his bloodstream, and the sharp stream from his most powerful tip could amputate.

But water isn't the only hazard of pressure washing: Darlington figures the safest ladder is the one he's not on. Six-foot wand extensions let him avoid soapy rungs by spraying from the ground; he'll fit on one or two to reach into gable ends and other awkward spots. It's an approach that requires vigilance, because the wobbly wand can smack windows or touch power lines. Whatever washer you buy or rent, take time to learn its nuances. If you rush into power washing, the way to a clean house will be littered with destruction.

[strippingpaint]

Stroking the 150-year-old columns

on the portico of a New England house, painter

JOHN DEE DUG INTO HIS POCKET FOR A KNIFE, POKED AT THE THICK coating and looked at Norm Abram. "15 or 20 coats of paint here?" "I'd say that's conservative," Norm replied. They inspected the rot in the base of the hollow column where water from a leaky roof had been collecting and shook their heads. Then Dee stood back, looked over what he termed "a very needy" project and saw something much more:

A subcontractor, Brooks Washburn, had to spray more than 20 gallons of semi-paste stripper on this portico. About 10 coats of paint came off on the first pass, and the rest came off on the second pass. Then came hours of laborious detail scraping by hand.

[stripping paint]

"A piece of fine exterior furniture." Although the portico would require a month of solid work and cost $6,000 to restore, Dee knew it would be worth the effort. "When you take a prominent space and treat it with impeccable craftsmanship, it makes for an impressive welcome to guests. In a neighborhood like this, you have to pamper the architecture, and the portico is the most significant architecture of this house."

when you *encounter a bulletproof layer of paint that resists all the chemical strippers you know of, try a heat gun instead: It can be an effective alternative.*

Such projects involve more than a few hours-worth of scraping with hand tools, however. Brooks Washburn used an expensive European-made system that pumps pure paint remover to the spray gun, where it is mixed with a very small amount of air. Brooks's father, Dick Washburn, president of the company that distributes the solvent-based stripper, says they prefer spraying it on to application with a brush or mop because it can be applied more evenly, less of the stripper gets on the user, and the air injected by the gun causes the stripper to foam, making it adhere better. As soon as the paint underneath started to wrinkle, the hard work of scraping—50 hours worth—began.

For sheer pleasure in the work, no renovation job gives less than scraping. It builds character, not happiness, and Dee will try any tool that works. To get into the horizontal groove near the top of each column, for example, Dee wrapped a cabinet scraper with sandpaper and pushed it into the slot. He says that the scratches produced by 100-grit paper are usually filled in by exterior primers, but to get an even smoother surface, he sanded the portico a second time with 150-grit paper. Even dental tools have a place in removing paint. "The most intricate architectural detailing on that portico is called *guttae*, Latin for 'drops,' he says of the fine carving on the frieze above the columns. "Dental tools were essential to get in there." He also uses a random-orbit sander (see page 14) on flat surfaces and to give a fine edge to the ribs on the columns.

Once paint has been removed with chemical strippers, Dee hand scrapes the wood to remove any paint residue that remains. He usually uses a hand scraping tool that has nine interchangeable blades of varying shapes and sizes.

After sanding, Dee repaired rotted wood at the base of each column. Finally, the surfaces were prepared with Swedish putty, a filler made in Holland of finely-ground

The true grace of architectural woodwork is revealed only when decades of paint no longer obscure the intricate details.

[strippingpaint]

remember:
It's paint removal you're after, not wood removal. Many people tend to over-scrape a surface. "Excavate paint, emancipate wood," says John Dee.

limestone and linseed oil. "It's remarkable stuff," says Dee. The limestone is ground so finely that it will fill an indentation as small as a pin scratch. He doesn't recommend it for any imperfection deeper than the thickness of a dime, however.

SCRAPING BY HAND

Not everyone is able to line up a spray-stripping system, however, and so hand-scraping is a common mechanism for separating paint from its host. *Scrape* may have an unpleasant onomatopoeic sound, but removing paint by hand sanding is slow and dusty, power sanding can erase details and leave gouges, and chemical stripping can be toxic. Together, a well-honed scraper and a pure heart can lead to ecstasies of scraping perfection, those heavenly moments when each stroke peels away long strips of encrusted paint to reveal the lovely wood hidden beneath. Anyone still scraping with grandfather's heirloom, however, will find this job tortuous, to say the least.

The secret of scraping is to use a variety of good modern tools, exceedingly sharp, some with wide blades that can peel the crud off in a single pass, others designed for narrow planes and tiny crevices where the corner of a wide one would do damage.

All paint scrapers are divided into two types: push and pull. The most common push scrapers look like double-wide putty knives with stiff blades designed to slip under and pop off loose paint. The best ones have full-

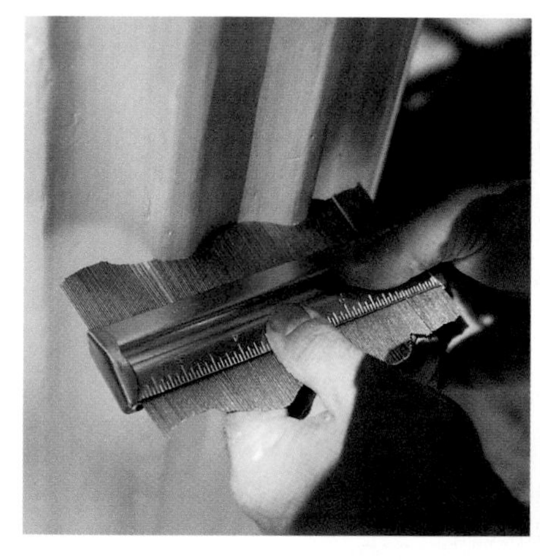

TECHNIQUES

Gauging: To further smooth surfaces after they were scraped, sanded and primed, Dee coated them with Swedish putty. First he used a contour gauge to match the pattern of the column ribs and flutes, then transferred the outline to a vinyl wallpaper smoother and cut it to fit with a utility knife, creating a custom putty spreader.

Mixing: Before applying the putty, Dee mixed it with a bit of tinting compound to make the putty easier to see against the paint primer. This extra step saves an enormous amount of time later on that would otherwise be spend scrutinizing the columns for each tiny bit of hardened filler prior to sanding.

Spreading: Dee squeegeed the putty onto the columns, torquing the wallpaper smoother a bit here and there so that it would conform to the irregularities of the wood.

Painting: After smoothing the Swedish putty with 150-grit sand-paper, Dee finished with two thin coats of paint. "It may seem like a lot of work, but if you think of it as exterior art, you see that it's worth it." The key characteristic of a great paint job, he adds, is paint that levels to a perfect smoothness.

[strippingpaint]

tang blades that go from the working edge to the handle (which can range from fairly standard to cleverly ergonomic) made of rubber, nylon or wood. Some push scrapers have hammering surfaces on the butt; others have screw sockets for poles to increase the reach. These work well for flooring adhesive, putty and caulk softened with a heat gun but they tend to nosedive into wood grain.

A pull scraper, on the other hand, can exert more downward thrust and sink the blade under the paint. The tool can go into the corners of tiny little reveals or scrape down bowling alleys with equal ease, and the blade can be switched to its sharper edge when it gets dull. Most modern pull scrapers have removable blades with two or more edges, in widths from 1 to 5 inches.

keep a scraper *blade honed by filing it every five minutes during heavy scraping. Maintain the scraper's straight edge; a concave edge will gouge wood.*

Blades held at an angle slightly toward the handle won't damage the wood as easily as blades held perpendicular to the wood. One type has two handles and eight interchangeable stainless-steel blades. They remain adequately sharp for a long time, and their curvaceous edges can scoop out the most intricate grooves, flutes and ogees from paint-smothered moldings.

The latest in pull-scraping technology is tungsten carbide, a harder-than-almost-anything alloy that saves a lot of blade filing.

A few "green" chemical paint strippers are based on nonflammable compounds and produce fewer toxic vapors. These products may work more slowly than traditional chemical strippers, but offer an alternative to other products.

The ads claim that carbide blades are two and a half times harder than the best steel, and that may be true. Of course, carbide replacement blades cost three times as much as steel and require a diamond-studded honing stone to touch up their edges. But in scraping, money spent is sweat saved.

When shopping for scrapers, trust your hands. If the manufacturer has shaped the handle scientifically to reduce fatigue, the tool will feel like an extension of your arm. Labels such as "contractor's grade" and "professional quality" sound nice, but "full warranty" is more reassuring.

« The secret of scraping is to use a variety of good modern tools, exceedingly sharp, some with wide blades that can peel the crud off in a single pass. »

To prepare flat surfaces (such as this door panel) for paint, Dee sometimes removes poorly adhered layers with a razor scraper before sanding the surface smooth. The blade should be replaced frequently; single-edge blades can be purchased inexpensively by the box from paint supply stores and from some tool catalogs.

[exteriorpainting]

SQUINTING AT A tiny droplet of wet paint on a window-sill, Andrew D'Amato grumbles and then steps back for the wide-angle view. "What's this?" he mutters as he spies a half dozen more all-but-invisible paint beads clinging to the window's casing. Striding around to the side of the house, he buttonholes the offending employee. "Front of the house, to the right of the door—drips!" he says tersely. The worker trots off obediently toward the scene of the crime, double-time, as D'Amato shakes his head.

when removing *shutters prior to painting, anticipate the presence of wasps or bats. Remove the shutters carefully and keep a can of bee spray ready.*

Among the many chores that humans tend to botch or rush, repainting a house's exterior must rank near the top. The word *slapdash*, denoting all acts hurried and shoddy, could have sprung precisely from the near-universal tendency to slap pigment on a weary clapboard, then dash off to do something more thrilling—pulling weeds, perhaps, or insulating a crawl space. While this tendency is regrettable, it's also understandable. The perfect visual metaphor for an endless, grueling task is a solitary house-painter staring up at a three-story Victorian replete with mildewed shingles, peeling muntins and alligatored filigree. Exhausting labor, dizzying heights and the specter of lead poisoning—no wonder average mortals blanch. But D'Amato, co-owner of Andrews Painting in Milton, Massachusetts, actually enjoys painting, and he cares deeply about tiny drips on a huge house. "Painting is the last step in the construction process and the most dramatic," he says. "The change we make is very satisfying.

Over the years, D'Amato, partner Andrew Lieberman and their crew have attended to dozens of grand old houses throughout greater Boston. "Our clients care about their homes," D'Amato says. "It's more to them than a place to plunk. It's a showpiece. That's why they love us."

A graduate of the Art Institute of Boston, he took up housepainting to repay school debts

House Rules. Painting craftsmen may argue with each other about the best tools, materials and techniques to use, but every one worth his overalls will agree on the importance of preparation. Before painters even look at a brush they invest time in readying a house for paint; there's more to it than just caulking joints (above) and tooling the goop smooth.

Many painters prefer the traditional 4-inch brush for applying paint; some prefer the speed of spray gear. Still others spray first, then work paint into the surface by brush.

[exterior painting]

and discovered his affinity for the work. Today's project is in Milton, at D'Amato's own house, which he and his wife began renovating three years earlier. With an expansive front porch and gorgeous fretwork, the circa-1865 house has awesome potential waiting beneath a striated, peeling, moldy, graying skin. "I'm sure it hasn't been painted since the '50s," he says.

Which made him eager to get started. But the first requirement of a paint job is patience. D'Amato never paints an exterior before June. "The long winters in New England saturate wood, especially exposed wood like this," he says. Atop a 24-foot ladder, he pulls a battery-operated moisture meter from a pocket and presses the meter's two prongs 1/4 inch into a clapboard high on the house's north side, the last spot to surrender its load of spring rain. "We like the moisture content to be under 12 percent. Here it's 10, so we're OK."

the weight *of a canvas dropcloth can kill flower borders. Use sawhorses and planks to support the cloth instead. Don't drape clear plastic over plants, either: the greenhouse you create can cook greenery.*

Time to paint? Not so fast. The most important single lesson to learn about top-notch housepainting is that more than half the job is not painting. "It's preparation," D'Amato says. "When we hire people, we tell them that prep is most of it. They say, 'Yeah, yeah, yeah, I know.' But as the days go by on the job, they say, 'I'm sick of this. I've got to paint something!'" D'Amato is generally an affable guy, but he never bends on this point. "I tell them, 'I think you need another job.'"

"It's like a toothache," says painter Andrew D'Amato of the bland, peeling paint of the "Before" version of his house. "Every time I look at it, it really bothers me." For a glimpse of the "After" version, see page 115.

On this sparkling June morning, D'Amato goes to the north side of his house, pulls off one of the abundant paint flakes and examines it. From its approximately 1/16-inch thickness, he guesses the house bears at least 10 coats. Because lead paint was not banned until 1978,

« **The most important** single lesson to learn about top-quality housepainting is that more than half the job is not painting: it's preparation. »

Tom Thevenin, wielding a garden sprayer, douses the house's north side with trisodium phosphate, bleach and water to vanquish dirt and to kill mold and mildew. D'Amato works the solution into the wood with a stiff brush.

[exteriorpainting]

all 10 layers may contain the toxic metal. To confine the aged paint he will remove, he unrolls a 20-foot-wide section of 6-mil-thick plastic and staples one edge of it to the bottom of the first course of clapboards. Then he and his crew prop up the tarp's edges with 1x8 boards, creating an 18-by-20-foot basin to catch debris.

Hand-scraping a huge house is only slightly more fun than a messy divorce, so power-tool manufacturers have tried for years to mechanize the chore. Of the half dozen tools available, all variations on the theme of a spinning cutter or grinder, D'Amato's choice for this job is called the Paint Shaver. A head with three triangular carbide scrapers can buzz off a full ⅛ inch from the clapboards, while a vacuum attachment keeps dust to a minimum. (Nonetheless, employee Tom Thevenin wears a respirator while working with the tool.) "The shaver is far from perfect; it's heavy, noisy, awkward and chews up the clapboard's surface pretty bad," D'Amato says. But the tool does strip paint right down to bare wood.

D'Amato concedes that he virtually never goes this far on other jobs—normally, he vigorously hand-scrapes and sands the remaining paint to round over sharp edges and promote adhesion. Strip-mining to reach bare wood is slow, expensive and unnecessary unless a house is experiencing massive paint failure, as his house is.

The mechanical stripper's bulk prevents it from removing paint within a couple of inches of trim such as corner boards. In these areas, D'Amato employs a heat gun, which softens the paint with hot air, so a handheld scraper can peel off layers like orange skin. His stripper can be adjusted to temperatures ranging from 250 to 1,100 degrees Fahrenheit, the maximum recommended by federal agencies to minimize the risk of vaporizing lead. To protect the wood and prevent fires,

protecting wood before painting

WHEN THE HISTORIC WOODEN FACADES OF DOWNTOWN LAFAYETTE, INDIANA, BEGAN TO PEEL AND ROT—LESS THAN FIVE YEARS AFTER BEING RESTORED—MICHAEL O. HUNT, A HISTORIC PRESERVATION BUFF WHO HEADS THE WOOD RESEARCH LABORATORY AT PURDUE UNIVERSITY, TOOK ACTION. IN THE FALL OF 1996 HE AND A CREW BUILT 279 MINIATURE "STOREFRONTS" AND TESTED 72 COMBINATIONS OF FIVE VARIABLES: TYPE OF WOOD, DESIGN, CAULK, WATER-REPELLENT PRESERVATIVES AND PAINT. AFTER 12 MONTHS OF EXPOSURE TO THE ELEMENTS, REPLICAS THAT HAD BEEN BRUSHED WITH PRESERVATIVE BEFORE PAINTING LOOKED VIRTUALLY UNSCATHED. BUT THOSE WITHOUT PRETREATMENT SPORTED CRACKED PAINT AND LOOSE JOINTS. TWO CAVEATS: APPLY THE REPELLENT BEFORE THE FIRST LICK OF PAINT OR PRIMER GOES ON, AND USE ONLY REPELLANTS LABELED "PAINTABLE".

he sets the thermostat at the lowest level that will do the job. Still, he says, "You want to wear a good-quality respirator with vapor cartridges."(See page 10 for more on respirators and other safety gear.)

With the wood bare, D'Amato patches missing post corners and other gaping wounds with a two-part wood-epoxy putty (see page 88.) "This stuff is fabulous," he says. "You just mold it and press it in place. You can fix almost anything with it."

Because the mechanical scraper roughed up the clapboards and the epoxy must be smoothed after it cures, the crew commences a double round of sanding using a disk sander with 36-grit paper followed by a random-orbit sander and 60-grit paper. "Strenuous and monotonous," D'Amato says, "but necessary."

But even the most assiduous scraping and sanding can't vanquish mold and mildew nestled in wood fibers. So D'Amato mixes a cleaning solution: a cup each of bleach and trisodium phosphate to 2 gallons of water. He sprays dirty and/or moldy surfaces and, after scrubbing with a stiff-bristled brush, allows everything to sit for half an hour while the bleach seeps in and destroys the invaders.

His final prep step is a gentle rinse with the hose to wash off paint dust, bleach and dead mold. "You have to rinse it— you don't want to mix all of that dust back in," says D'Amato. Unlike some painters, he prefers not

Sometimes it's easier to work on a house by carefully removing parts of it. Shutters (left) and latticework panels (right) can usually be detached for cleaning and spray-painting, reducing long stays on a ladder.

[exteriorpainting]

to use a pressure washer (see page 94). Other painters might disagree, claiming that the tool is great if used carefully, but few deny that there's a risk in using it. "You can write your name in a clapboard with a power washer. They're great for masonry, but I would never use one on wood," says D'Amato.

A HIDDEN LAYER OF PROTECTION

On D'Amato's 3,000-square-foot, two-story house, all of this preparation takes the four-man crew two weeks. But finally, after the rinse water dries, comes the moment: The brushes are brought out triumphantly, and the first coat goes on: water repellent.

Bad painters brush paint on bare wood. Good painters prime first. But D'Amato and other excellent painters follow the recommendation of the Forest Products Laboratory in Madison, Wisconsin—they pretreat bare wood with a clear, paintable water repellent to keep the siding from absorbing moisture that gets past the paint (see "Protecting wood before painting," page 110).

Manufacturers of wooden windows and doors have a secret: Coating bare wood with a paintable water-repellent preservative keeps paint on longer. Now, D'Amato and a few other top-of-the-line painters are borrowing the trick, which is backed up by research at Purdue University as well as at the Forest

evaluating old paint

THE CONDITION OF PAINT ON A HOUSE, AS WELL AS THE HEALTH OF THE WOOD BENEATH IT, ARE YOUR BEST CLUES TO FIGURING OUT HOW MUCH WORK LIES AHEAD.

INSPECT THE PAINT FOR CRACKS. NUMEROUS HORIZONTAL AND VERTICAL FISSURES SIGNAL THAT OIL-BASED PAINT IS LOSING ITS GRIP AND MUST BE REMOVED. WHEN THE BUILDUP IS MORE THAN 1/16 INCH THICK, AS IT IS HERE, SHEER WEIGHT IS PART OF THE PROBLEM. "THERE'S JUST TOO MUCH PAINT ON THIS PLACE," SAYS ANDREW D'AMATO.

LOOK FOR GRAY WOOD. PROLONGED EXPOSURE TO THE WEATHER TURNS WOOD GRAY, AND WEATHERED WOOD MAKES A POOR BASE FOR NEW PAINT. BECAUSE SUNLIGHT DEGRADES THE LIGNIN THAT HOLDS WOOD CELLS TOGETHER, SURFACE FIBERS NO LONGER BOND TO THE WOOD UNDERNEATH. NEW PAINT WILL STICK—BUT JUST TO A SURFACE THAT'S ABOUT TO BE SLOUGHED OFF. PEELING WILL REAPPEAR.

BRIGHT WOOD CAN BE GOOD NEWS. UNDERNEATH ALL THE GUNK IS WOOD THAT LOOKS AS GOOD AS NEW, AND IT MAY BE EVEN BETTER AT HOLDING PAINT THAN MODERN CLAPBOARDS ARE. OLD CLAPBOARDS OFTEN CAME FROM TREES THAT GREW SLOWLY AND WERE RIFT-SAWN TO MINIMIZE WARP.

Products Laboratory. It's important that the label of a wood preservative make three claims: "water repellent," "preservative" and "paintable." The water repellent, often a wax, keeps the wood from shrinking or swelling as much when it rains, so the paint stretches less, stays intact and grips the wood longer. The preservative kills mildew, which could grow into the top paint layer and ruin its look, and fungi that cause wood to rot.

There is a wide variation in formulas on the market, however. To find an effective preservative, follow the lead of the many window and door manufacturers who use products that contain 3-iodo-2-propynyl butylcarbamate, an iodine-based preservative often abbreviated IPBC. (Preservatives are usually listed on labels.) Repellents not labeled "paintable" may contain so much wax that paint won't stick. When in doubt, test first in an inconspicuous area. "After the paint is dry, press a piece of adhesive tape on it," says Alan Ross, vice president and technical director for Wolman Wood Care Products, which makes water-repellent preservatives. "When you pull it up, does it pull up the paint? Compare it to an area where you haven't put the repellent."

Looking for problems. Reading peeling paint as a pointer to moisture problems, D'Amato spots a leaking wooden gutter above the worst-looking shutter. He presses lead flashing into the gutter's seams, secures the metal with brass tacks and then seals the edges with roofing asphalt.

FINALLY, THE PAINT

After the repellent dries, D'Amato's crew masks windows with blue painter's tape and builder's paper and applies an oil-based primer. "We spray it on, then brush it out," says D'Amato, expertly sweeping and stabbing with a natural-bristle brush to work the wet primer into cracks and crevices. He prefers oil-based primers because they penetrate better than latexes do. The primer, however, raises the grain. So D'Amato's crew smooths the dried film with light passes of a palm sander fitted with 100-grit paper, then sweeps off the resulting dust with a soft-bristled shop brush. (For more on primers, see pages 74-81.)

In the course of 133 years, D'Amato's house has collected cracks, crevices and dings, which are unsightly and accelerate leaks and rot. So he guns on 25-year latex-acrylic caulk, patrolling every square foot of the exterior. He seals around trim but leaves cracks between

[exteriorpainting]

clapboards, so moisture can escape from the house's interior; if the whole exterior were sealed tightly, migrating moisture could make the paint bubble and peel off the walls.

Caulking finished, D'Amato sprays on another coat of primer. "Now all of the caulk is sealed between two coats of primer. It's not essential, but at this point it's easy—you've already got the sprayer out and the windows masked off, so why not?"

Finally, the painter actually paints. After all of the prep work, this long-awaited metamorphosis seems almost instantaneous. "We just spray it on. The surface is already perfectly smooth, so there is no need to brush it in." D'Amato applies two coats of flat latex. A sprayed-on coat is thicker than a brushed coat, and some paint is lost to overspray, so a gallon covers about 250 square feet instead of the usual 500. D'Amato sprays as lightly as possible, in keeping with this rule: Two thin coats are more durable than a single thick one.

He paints the body of the house first, then progresses to the trim, brushing on two coats of an appealing glossy off-white around doors and windows. "I always go with an oil-based paint for the trim coat," he says. "I like its sheen. You can work it longer. You don't have to worry about it drying up and leaving ugly lap marks." The choice of oil paint or latex paint, however, is one that often depends on the existing paint surface (see page 74.)

In all, D'Amato and his team will spread and spray 53 gallons of paint and finishes on this house: 8 gallons of sealer, 15 gallons of primer, 15 gallons of the siding paint, 12 gallons of trim paint and 3 gallons of deep green on the shutters. Total paint cost: $1,530. If he were charging a client, D'Amato estimates the total for materials and labor would come in at about $20,000. "The scraping to bare wood is what really elevates that price," he says. A less vigorous scrape could drop the cost by half, to as little as $10,000.

As the sprayer's compressor groans and the last coat hisses into place, D'Amato's affinity for his craft suddenly makes perfect sense. Once forlorn, just another big old Boston-area house gone to seed, the Victorian is now breathtaking.

Sweaty, rumpled and dappled with paint, D'Amato shades his eyes and takes a long, loving look at the flawless facade. "This is not a color change," he says. "This is a transformation."

Spraying siding. D'Amato uses an airless sprayer on clapboards, which pumps paint fast (but wastes some in overspray). For detail work such as lattice, he switches to a HVLP sprayer (see page 68) because it is more accurate.

try not to

paint walls while they are exposed to direct sunlight, especially in summer months. The sun's heat can cause paint to blister.

Although his painters sprayed most of the clapboards, D'Amato contends there's no substiture for brushwork near the trim. "You need that control," he says, underscoring his philosophy that the best way to paint a house is also the easiest: "If I just slapped some paint on, every other year I would be chasing it, touching it up. With the kind of job we can do, we get seven to 10 years out of a job."

[historic paints]

BEFORE PAINT CAME IN a can, tinted with precise squirts of universal colorants dispensed by machine, it was mixed one batch at a time from materials that mostly came from the earth. To folks who wonder what their old houses might have looked like when new, that's a handy fact. Know what once went into paint, and you'll see why certain colors simply were not available. You'll also realize that no precise list of historic colors is "correct." Intensity and tone varied according to how the pigments were made, how the proportions were mixed and even how hard the painter was willing to work.

tiny chips *of color from the paint store can be deceiving. Once you've found colors you might like, buy a quart of each and paint small areas of the house. Take a look from curbside and adjust as needed.*

One of the last working ocher mines in the United States, for example, is in Georgia, and sometimes yields a different color each foot. And Prussian blue gets darker the more it is ground or brushed. Maybe it was painter fatigue that resulted in each of the blue rooms at Mount Vernon turning out a different shade. George Washington was not pleased—he wrote a note to that effect—but for people like Deborah and Kevin Guinee, such news could be a liberating revelation. They had to select colors to use in painting their half-Federal, half-Victorian house in Salem, Massachusetts, the centerpiece of a *This Old House* broadcast. They could select colors they like, secure in the knowledge that within certain limits, anything from bright to pastel could be historically appropriate. "Painting," observed one historic paint expert, "was the art of the possible."

Some years ago, *This Old House* viewers watched as Chris Hagger went before the Wayland Historic District Commission for permission to return his family's house to the colors it wore in 1888: medium yellow with trim in cream and shutters in park-bench green. Some at the meeting in the small Massachusetts town were aghast. "When people think about New England and New England house colors, they think white," noted one resident. Maybe "something softer," urged a commissioner, suggesting that medium yellow was "too intense a color for such an enormous structure." Finally Hagger was asked whether he actually liked the color scheme, revealed in a laboratory analysis by

Traditional paint: Old paint made with yellow and red ocher and red lead crusts buckets in Eastfield Village's historical collection. Red lead was sometimes called minium, and when mixed with oil, it became a fast-drying primer.

Paint made from natural pigments covers Georg Kremer's house in Aichstetten, Germany. The richness of traditional American natural-pigment colors can be every bit as surprising.

« The invention of synthetic pigments is what really opened up a whole rainbow of options—and at the same time, unfortunately, began to close some doors. »

GEORGIA EARTH: Colorful dirt like this was once used as the base colorant for yellow ocher paint.

[historicpaints]

the Society for the Preservation of New England Antiquities. "Um...," he said. But asked again, he replied: "I like the colors. If this were not a historical renovation project, there are other colors I might consider."

obsession
over color selection is common. When it gets burdensome, however, you might be able to hire an architect or building designer to help out.

Many people probably have a similar reaction to the reds, browns, olive greens and mustard yellows that have been painted on some historically correct restorations of 18th- and 19th-century buildings (the examples below are in Historic Deerfield Village, Massachusetts). They might feel differently if they talked to Georg Kremer, Ph.D., a chemist in Germany who has spent years searching out the pits that once supplied pigments to Europe and early North America. In fact, they'd probably be stunned by pictures of his home, protected with a lime-based paint he made from natural pigments. But many would probably find the suprising colors far more pleasing than some of the present-day attempts at recreating old colors.

Of course, there's more to choosing paint than picking a likable color; the gloss (or lack of it) can have profound effects. Chris Ohrstrom is president of Historic Paints Ltd., a company in East Meredith, New York, that sells interior paints made with linseed oil and mostly traditional pigments. Above his paint lab is an 1830s tavern that he restored. Woodwork brushed with his company's paint glows with a soft sheen that is remarkable, a testament to the difference texture can make.

And then there's Eastfield Village, a collection of old buildings assembled by Don Carpentier over the past 20 years on what used to be his father's "east field" in East Nassau, New York. Every summer, restoration experts and other curious folks show up to take classes in old-time building skills at Carpentier's school of historic construction

The earliest houses, like the Parson Jonathan Ashley house of 1733, were often bare. The traces of white here date to the 1830s.

This 1765 saltbox is painted in minium, or red lead color. The windows are white; the door is painted gray.

When exteriors were painted, trim came first. Venetian red protects sash at the 1743 Sheldon-Hawks house.

The Bardwell-Humphrey house of 1771 has a putty color appropriate to the period. The original color of the house isn't known.

techniques. In a paint class, Matthew Mosca, an adviser to Historic Paints, demonstrated how to grind and grind and grind to get pigment particles small enough to mesh with oil (see page 120). Given that chore, it was easy to see why most interior walls used to be painted instead with water-based paints. Mosca stirred up a quantity of milk, lime, linseed oil, chalk and bone black to make pale gray paint for the upper walls of a room in an Eastfield tavern building. An earlier class had already painted the room's lower walls with a glue-based light pink. Both colors dried matte and somewhat streaky—just what Carpentier wanted. This kind of technique, something less than factory perfect, could easily be made even more beautiful.

Most people, though, aren't about to make their own paint. They want nonstreaky, fast-drying stuff that comes in a can. "Latex acrylic does really great things," paint expert Frank Welsh says. "In my own house, it's what I'd use." But what color? One way to answer this question is to hire someone like Welsh or Mosca. For a fee, they'll search for and remove undisturbed paint blobs and examine them under a microscope. They'll determine whether the bottom paint layer was the first on the house—or just the first since it was last stripped—and whether it is a faded or yellowed version of some originally brighter color. (Analyzing a submitted sample, says Welsh, is less expensive.) With luck you'll end up like Hagger did, with color swatches a paint store can match. The other way to choose color is to learn something about exterior paint styles and paint materials and then just wing it.

The earliest homes in America were bare outside. By the 1700s, color had become common in cities but was still rare in the

Resin, the pitch of various conifers, was once dissolved in different solvents to make varnish and added to oil paint to make enamel. Clockwise from top right: Manila copal, damar, mastic, sandarac, elemi. Sandarac and some copals were dissolved in alcohol, other copals in oil, and mastic in turpentine.

The Hinsdale and Anna Williams house, white with green shutters after an 1817 remodeling, has a gilded fanlight above the door.

The front door surround of the David Dickinson house (1783) dates to the 1800s. The fanlight was painted black to hide second-floor framing behind it.

Houses often had stylish colors in front, cheap Spanish brown in back, as on the Joseph Barnard house of 1768.

This is how the Wells-Thorn house looked in the 1800s: The original 1725 wing is bare, while the 1751 addition is light sky blue.

[historicpaints]

countryside. Bright colors prevailed before the Revolution, gradually giving way to lighter colors after the war. By the 1830s, serene and timeless Greek Revival white was the norm, even in the countryside. Softer earth colors came into vogue in the mid-1800s, and by the Victorian period, dark green and dark brown were the fashion. Interestingly, the paint palette varied little among the colonies, regardless of whether they were tied to England, Spain, France or even Russia. A bishop's house, for example, in Sitka, Alaska, was painted mostly in yellow ocher, a color derived from iron oxide.

Even after paint began to be sold in cans in the 1860s, many painters mixed their own. And whether found in a can or mixed from scratch, the ingredients were mostly what they had been through the ages. The invention of synthetic pigments is what really opened up a whole rainbow of options—and at the same time, unfortunately, began to close some doors. No longer do most people have any idea of what goes into paint, or any thought that they can adapt it as they like. Instead, they invariably turn to premixed colors.

During one break at Eastfield, someone asked Carpentier about the possibility of mixing some of the old pigments into modern paints as a way of getting the best of both worlds. As it turned out, that's just what he had done inside another building. The walls were white latex, with a little bone black mixed in. "Guess what?" he said of the strategy. "It was fun."

TECHNIQUES

Pigment: The traditional pigment Prussion blue is available today, as it was in the 1700s. Here, pigment is dumped on a stone slab such as those used for centuries to mix paint.

Linseed oil: Paint expert Matthew Mosca shows how powdered pigment turns into paint. First, he adds boiled linseed oil, a binder pressed from the seeds of the flax plant. Linseed oil binds any suspended pigments to the surface below. With a putty knife, materials are blended to a paste.

The mixture: After Mosca hand-grinds the paste using a stone muller to meld oil and pigment, the finished blue is ready; it will be added to a white paint base.

Blending paints: Mosca gradually adds blue to a bowl of white titanium dioxide paint and stirs, scrutinizing each deepening shade of color until he reaches the one he's after. Like a traditional Prussion blue, the final paint may change color on a wall as it responds to the painter's brushstrokes.

paint chart

EARTH-BASED PIGMENTS

BURNT UMBER: Umber is a dull brown or greenish-brown clay when dug. It contains an iron oxide (thus its reddish tint) and a manganese oxide (the source of its brown). Umber was often painted on trim in Georgian paneled rooms or combed on doors to simulate mahogany grain.

VENETIAN RED: Venetian red was one common name for earth rich in iron oxide. It provided the "barn red" so popular for exteriors. The iron ore shown here came from France.

SPANISH BROWN: Spanish brown was made from a variety of iron oxides less brilliant than those in Venetian red, including red jasper, hematite and red earth from Tuscany. It was used as a primer and as a cheap finish coat.

TERRE VERTE: French for "green earth," terre verte was made from a variety of rocks long thought to contain copper. Now we know the color comes from iron silicate. Somewhat drab and transparent, terre verte was mostly replaced after the mid-1800s by a mix of chrome yellow and Prussian blue.

YELLOW OCHER: Yellow ocher is the most common iron oxide. Often tinged with brown or orange, it was sold under a variety of names, including French ocher. Popular for walls and trim inside and out, it could also be mixed with white to make straw, stone or cream colors.

ORGANIC PIGMENT

COCHINEAL: Made from female cochineal bugs, which feed on the prickly pear cactus. Prized from Mexico to Peru before the Spanish arrived. Used mostly as a dye. Still used in cosmetics.

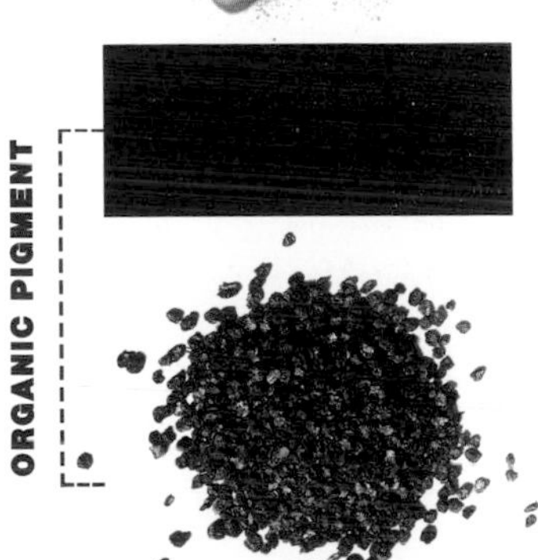

PROCESSED PIGMENTS

MINIUM: French for red lead. Though a naturally occuring lead oxide, it was usually prepared by roasting white lead or litharge, a yellow oxide of lead. Boiled with the linseed oil for other paints, it made them dry faster. It was often used to finish cabinet interiors.

CHROME YELLOW: Crocoite, naturally occurring lead chromate, was discovered in 1770. Chemists then worked to make it artificially. The pigment went on sale in 1818 and within two years was in common use.

PRUSSIAN BLUE: The first synthetic pigment, popular inside and out as a status symbol. Invented about 1704 by a Prussian pharmacist who worked for years to replicate a reaction that had once turned his trash pile blue.

VERDIGRIS: Verdigris is corroded copper. For paint, copper sheets were exposed to vinegar fumes for weeks, then crystals were scraped off. Verdigris darkened with age.

WHITE LEAD: Lead carbonate was often used in oil paints because it coated well and stayed flexible. Relatively costly, it was made by suspending lead pieces over vinegar in pots, which were then stacked with manure or tanbark for heat and left for about two months. This produced white crystals that could be removed, broken up and ground with oil.

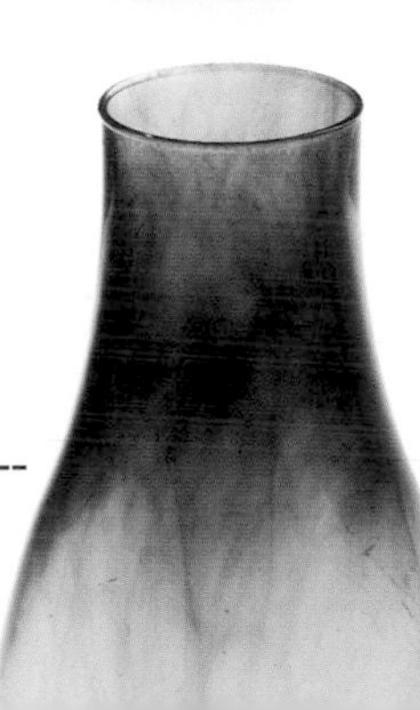

LAMP BLACK: Lampblack is nothing more than the soot from incompletely burned oil. Made in hooded furnaces, it was fine and somewhat greasy. It mixed well with linseed oil but not with water-based paints. Those usually called for bone black, made from animal bones burned in a closed container.

[historicpaints]

***

PAINT ARCHEOLOGY

SHE CAME ARMED WITH A RAZOR-EDGED STAINLESS-STEEL SCALPEL. When architectural conservator Andrea Gilmore went treasure hunting at a *This Old House* project in Milton, Massachusetts, she headed for a corner of the facade and ran her fingers across a clapboard that had been nailed in place nearly 300 years ago. Then, with one precise stroke, she took a slice.

authenticity *has its place, but the color scheme of a house should reflect the well-advised personal preferences of its current owners.*

Carving through multiple layers of paint, she shaved off a sliver of white pine less than ½ inch long. Gilmore's eventual treasure haul—nearly two dozen paint-covered slivers delicately extracted from clapboards, shutters and window trim—looked to the naked eye like a small pile of construction detritus. But when viewed in cross section under a microscope and magnified 75 times, each tiny sliver presented a panoramic view of the house's history as layer after layer of color unfolded across the miniature screen. Gilmore discovered that the house had been painted 20 times during the past three centuries. "The color schemes trace the history of typical paint styles in this country," she says. The paint choices also reflect the idiosyncrasies of the house's owners over the years and occasionally raise the question: What on earth were those folks thinking?

In part, they were thinking about what was available. When farmer John Crehore built the house in the 1720s, he blanketed the clapboards in a thick layer of dark brown paint and detailed the window trim in russet. Crehore apparently was a man of austere tastes, but the dreary brown also happened to be one of the few colors available to him. House painters of the day carried their own ingredients and mixed paint on-site. Earth colors—reds, browns, yellows, grays and tans—dominated because their pigments were easy to find. "Technology drives style," says Robert Schweitzer, adjunct professor of architectural history at Eastern Michigan University in Ypsilanti.

Crehore's grandson, John, added a new wing and used lead paint to render the house pristine white. Clearly, the times were a-changing. "The American Revolution—and the notion that we were one of the only countries in the world without a king—had created a fascination with the Greek city-state," says Schweitzer. "White was the color of the day because it emulated the marble and stone found in Greek temples."

On the eve of the Civil War, mechanization transformed the paint industry. "It was the beginning of paint in a can," says Gilmore. Color choices multiplied and the house, like many others loved by generations, saw a succession of colors.

Investigating Paint: Using a razor-edged stainless-steel scalpel (1), Gilmore deftly seizes a sliver of paint from a window casing that had been protected by a porch since the early 1800s.

A magnified sliver of the paint (2) shows 1720s pine casing at left, plus 20 layers of paint. A practiced eye can identify individual layers.

When a house carries so many layers of paint, it's up to solvent-baset chemicals to strip them away (3). After the layers have been excavated, subtle details hidden for decades emerge from the woodwork.

* * *

CREDITS

AUTHORS: Thomas Baker, Susan Benesch, Jill Connors, Mark Feirer, Jeff Hosking, Jeanne Huber, Peter Jensen, Brad Lemley, Bill Marsano, James Morgan, Stephen L. Petranek, Romy Pokorny, Curtis Rist, Victoria Rowan, John Saladyga, Wendy Talarico and Jeff Taylor.

PHOTOGRAPHERS: Melanie Acevedo, Greg Anthon, David Barry, Matthew Benson, John Bentham, Pascal Blancon, Peter Bosch, Chris Buck, Anthony Cotsifas, Jim Cooper, Bill Geddes, Michael Grimm, Darrin Haddad, Spencer Jones, Keller & Keller, John Kernick, Michael McLaughlin, Michael Myers, Benjamin Oliver, Anna Palma, David Prince, Kolin Smith, Wayne Sorce, William Vazquez and James Worrell. Additional photographs courtesy of Rohm & Haas.

ILLUSTRATIONS: Bob Hambly

THIS OLD HOUSE® BOOKS

EDITOR: Mark Feirer

CREATIVE DIRECTOR: Matthew Drace

ART DIRECTOR: Dina White

ART ASSOCIATE: Matthew Bates

PRODUCTION ASSOCIATE: Duane Stapp

COPY EDITOR: Melanie Bush

PAINTING CONSULTANT: John Dee

DIRECTOR, NEW PRODUCT DEVELOPMENT: Bob Fox

ASSISTANT PRODUCT MANAGER: Miriam Silver

SPECIAL THANKS TO: Norm Abram, Steve Thomas, Tom Silva, Richard Trethewey, Bruce Irving and Russell Morash at the show; Betsy Groban and Peter McGhee at WGBH; Stephen VanHove and Anthony Wendling at Applied Graphics Technology; Robert Hardin; and Chris "Scanman" Kwieraga and Michele "Photofinder" Fleury at *This Old House* magazine.

Funding for *This Old House* on public television is provided by State Farm Insurance Companies, Ace Hardware Corporation and The Minwax & Krylon Brands.

« The most important way station on the journey to painting excellence is proper preparation. »

[recording your colors]

MORE THAN A FEW PAINT-READY HOME OWNERS HAVE faltered, intimidated by the sheer number of colors any paint store can mix. Don't despair. First, know that 2½ square inches of paint on a chip can't accurately mimic 130 square feet of painted bedroom wall. Your perception of color is affected by the type of light you see it in, by how much of it you're looking at and even by the colors nearby. In order to choose a color, then, buy 1 quart of a likely prospect, and paint two coats on large scraps of drywall or plywood. When the paint dries, prop your sample flat against a wall, and stand back to scrutinize it. Check it in daylight, twilight and at night with the room lights on. Can you live with it? A wasted quart isn't nearly as expensive as a whole room painted wrong, so paint more samples if you must. Record the details of your rooms on these pages, and attach the successful paint chips for a permanent record of your choices, where they went and how much paint you needed.

ROOM

WALLS S.F.

CEILING S.F.

TRIM L.F.

OTHER

attcah paint chip here

ROOM

WALLS S.F.

CEILING S.F.

TRIM L.F.

OTHER

attach paint chip here

ROOM

WALLS S.F.

CEILING S.F.

TRIM L.F.

OTHER

attach paint chip here

ROOM

WALLS S.F.

CEILING S.F.

TRIM L.F.

OTHER

attach paint chip here

attach paint chip here

ROOM

WALLS S.F.

CEILING S.F.

TRIM L.F.

OTHER

attach paint chip here

ROOM

WALLS S.F.

CEILING S.F.

TRIM L.F.

OTHER

attach paint chip here

ROOM

WALLS S.F.

CEILING S.F.

TRIM L.F.

OTHER

attach paint chip here

ROOM

WALLS S.F.

CEILING S.F.

TRIM L.F.

OTHER

[recordingyourcolors]

WALLS S.F.
TRIM L.F.
TRIM L.F.
WINDOW SASH NUMBER
DOORS NUMBER
OTHER

attach paint chip here

WALLS S.F.
TRIM L.F.
TRIM L.F.
WINDOW SASH NUMBER
DOORS NUMBER
OTHER

attach paint chip here

WALLS S.F.
TRIM L.F.
TRIM L.F.
WINDOW SASH NUMBER
DOORS NUMBER
OTHER

attach paint chip here

WALLS S.F.
TRIM L.F.
TRIM L.F.
WINDOW SASH NUMBER
DOORS NUMBER
OTHER

attach paint chip here